JE T'AIME

JE T'AIME

The legendary love story of
Jane Birkin and Serge Gainsbourg

VÉRONIQUE MORTAIGNE

TRANSLATED BY GEORG PHILIPP VON PEZOLD

ICON

Published in the UK in 2019
by Icon Books Ltd, Omnibus Business Centre,
39–41 North Road, London N7 9DP
email: info@iconbooks.com
www.iconbooks.com

Sold in the UK, Europe and Asia
by Faber & Faber Ltd, Bloomsbury House,
74–77 Great Russell Street,
London WC1B 3DA or their agents

Distributed in the UK, Europe and Asia
by Grantham Book Services, Trent Road, Grantham NG31 7XQ

Distributed in the USA
by Publishers Group West,
1700 Fourth Street, Berkeley, CA 94710

Distributed in Australia and New Zealand
by Allen & Unwin Pty Ltd,
PO Box 8500, 83 Alexander Street,
Crows Nest, NSW 2065

Distributed in South Africa
by Jonathan Ball, Office B4, The District,
41 Sir Lowry Road, Woodstock 7925

Distributed in India by Penguin Books India,
7th Floor, Infinity Tower – C, DLF Cyber City,
Gurgaon 122002, Haryana

Distributed in Canada by Publishers Group Canada,
76 Stafford Street, Unit 300
Toronto, Ontario M6J 2S1

ISBN: 978-178578-484-2

Typeset in Granjon by Marie Doherty

Printed and bound in Great Britain
by Clays Ltd, Elcograf S.p.A.

Contents

Jane, Serge and Régine share a joke in Deauville, Normandy, 1969
(PHOTO: ANDREW BIRKIN)

one

Cresseveuille

I n the afternoon, I drove up the D 675 to Cresseveuille. At that moment my thoughts couldn't have been further away from Gonzague Saint Bris. An eccentric journalist, right-wing admirer of Louis XI, he had crossed the alps on the back of a mule in order to emulate Leonardo da Vinci, having previously founded the very swanky *Academie Romantique*, a cultural group of high-profile French intellectuals.

That 8 August, in 2017, at the age of 69, the fashionable writer died in the old-fashioned way: the car wrapped around a tree on the D 675, which links Rouen to Caen, the romanticism of Cabourg to the horse tracks of Deauville.

I am a woman of the coast, of pearl greys and blurred blues: they illuminate the sea of Normandy. I distrust the dense hinterland, with its leafy calm, its ponds that threaten to drown you, its thatch – at the mercy of rot. And yet, I have ventured inland. I have come to visit Cresseveuille. Like a return to the scene of the crime. It was here that Jane and Serge spent holidays with their daughters.

In December 1971, the young Gonzague Saint Bris is 23 years old. He publishes one of his first articles in *Le Figaro*, entitled 'Gainsbourg has reached his cherry season'. The middle of life's journey. Gainsbourg, then 43, is as ripe as a Morello cherry in the sun. He sings: a derisive cockerel. Gainsbourg, Saint Bris writes, is the epitome of a 'commercial' artist: he sprinkles his lyrics with brand names, with Guerlain perfume and advertisements for aperitifs. 'Gainsbourg is not hand-some, to say the least. But he has done what should be done in such a case: elevate ugliness to an art form. A difficult under-taking that he has mastered as he will master many others: with ease.'

Gonzague Saint Bris errs in one respect. Nothing had been easy. The whole endeavour might have capsized if Gainsbourg hadn't met Jane Birkin in May 1968. The leafy green of Normandy was the backdrop to his metamorphosis. This is where he became beautiful. The transformation took time. It took several seasons to develop.

Gainsbourg has spent lots of time in Normandy with his family. During the pre-war years, they roamed the beaches in the summer. Joseph, his father, made a living playing the piano in casino bars. In 1975, Jane, his young English lover and the mother of his daughter Charlotte, buys a house in Cresseveuille, at a stretch of the D 675, the fatal route where Gonzague Saint Bris' partner tried to avoid an animal before going off the road. In this Normandy, descended from Viking heathens, some might detect the hand of the *'Dames Blanches'* – the local female spirits – and other creatures of a parallel world, which has been transformed by Christian fervour over the centuries into a cauldron of punishment and devilments.

It was Régine, the 'Queen of the Night', who, in 1968, played good fairy to that happiness born in Normandy. With her, Serge enjoys memorable fits of laughter. 'Régine had bought a house near Honfleur' the photographer Tony Frank, who was there (throughout the 'mythical' couple's love story) relates. Serge, Jane and her daughter Kate in the grass, entwined bodies and conspiring glances: Tony Frank is a player. He sees every-thing, accompanies them everywhere. They are beautiful. They occasionally spend the day at the seaside, a big crowd gathered around Jane's entertaining brother Andrew. 'They were in love like infatuated youngsters, they played about like kittens.' This inspires legendary photos, and bags of memories. 'Régine takes out a used bottle of Martini wrapped in newspaper. It was moonshine calvados from the local bootlegger. Chess is being played, the bottle gets emptied, then another. I took them to a station – I don't remember which one.' Tony Frank, formerly a fellow-traveller of the Hallyday tribe, still sports – even today – the iodised tan of celebrity photographers.

Jane uses the money she made in 1974 from Claude Zizi's film *I'm Losing My Temper* to buy 'an impossibly pretty little vicarage, perched next to the church, nothing Norman about it; a slate roof, I've added a storey and a toilet.' The escapades with friends and family end in Deauville, *Chez Miocque*: a restaurant displaying signed celebrity photos on the walls, offering fish of the day and apple tart, or at the bar of the *Normandy*, invariably cosy, with its collection of rare whiskies and sporting pictures.

A picture, signed 'Siss', hangs prominently in the left hand corner above the best table for observing the comings and goings of celebrities. It depicts the Gainsbarre of depression: an empty gaze, he is alone with his bitch Nana. Stubble, white ballet shoes and jeans. Cigarette butts litter the floor; he plays the organ grinder, makes a performing dog dance with no spectators other than a couple of pigeons. It took some melancholy to shatter that joy! In ten years, everything has broken down. Cresseveuille was where the seeds that would destroy that happiness were planted. Serge Gainsbourg changed from an insouciant with a twig between his teeth, from a mischievous doting father, to 'Gainsbarre', drinker of '102': a double measure of Pastis 51.

Jane Birkin loved her vicarage 'between cemetery and motor-way, with rusty crosses and all.' It is gone. Gainsbourg has lost. Jane cleared off to the department of Finistère, to Lannilis, where Serge's father had supported the French Resistance. All that remains of the house of Norman happiness is a grey wall and a light signal above a great gate that was meant to flash when visitors came and went, but which is now permanently off. It is attached to the Church of Notre Dame de l'Assomption, whose foundations were laid in the flinty ground during the 13th century and whose wooden nave is like an upside-down boat, with its adjacent wash house.

Everything about the couple's life in the Norman village has already been said. Yes, Serge went shopping on his Solex moped, for drinks at Gerard's, in the village of Danestal, or at Anni's at Beaufour-Druval. Yes, we have glimpsed one of the *Magnificent Seven*, the actor Yul Brynner: a handsome and mysterious Russian Jew with a shaved head. Surrogate godfather to Charlotte, he came for neighbourly visits from his mansion at Bonnebosq, some fifteen kilometres away. An octogenarian farmer confides that he often drank with the singer, while another neighbour claims that his drinking bouts didn't last too long, adding that he 'was a good family man'. He laughed with the children and worked at night.

When Serge and Jane return to Paris, they entrust the house to a local farmer they befriended, René Touffet, aka 'Toto'. We are not going to get to the bottom of the enigma in this way.

The magic of Jane and Serge, a unique presence, a couple united by happenstance and need, reveals itself only in details. It's the parts that make the whole. For such sensitive, thin-skinned individuals, leaving for a small Norman village couldn't have been without meaning.

The D 675 is dangerous, as everybody knows. It used to be a trunk road, shoving itself into the Pays d'Auge, where the greenery hides more than just apple trees, cows and calvados. Closer to the sea, everything, or almost everything, ends in 'ville': Trouville, Deauville, Benerville, Tourgéville, Blonville. However, in the woodland retreat where the couple had decided to spend their summers, it's a different kettle of fish. All along the D 675 sleepy towns with strange names are nestling: le Petit-malheur, la Haie-tondue, la Queue-devée, la Forge, le Calvaire …

Water is abundant at Cresseveuille, whose name derives from 'watercress'. In the depths of the woods a different story lies hidden ... Their dangers aren't spread out evenly, one just brushes up against them. You need a real talent to recognise them, and a kind of sideways curiosity. A hoodlum of the first order, Gainsbourg explored the fringes. Jane, all innocence, was ready for any experience.

I have crossed the river Touques, the seaside version of the boundary that separates the right bank and the left bank in Paris. I finish my dinner at the *Central* in Trouville – salted fried shrimps, *blanche de Normandie* (a kind of calvados) for digestion. I think of the paper napkins on which a love-struck Gainsbourg used to draw elegant sketches of Jane, Charlotte and Kate, in an effort to slow the passage of time that was about to accelerate. 'Gainsbourg was born during the era of the *Brasserie Lip*,* at the height of the 20th century, in the wind, into a life that he preferred to fill with speed, showy cars and fast music that can be quantified' wrote Saint Bris, all white shirt and windswept hair. Our time is limited and, bizarrely, one is usually bored. The *Poinçonneur des Lilas*, the Ticket-Puncher at

---

*   A café on the left bank; one of the famous Saint Germain meeting places (among them the *Flore* or the *Deux Magots*) of Parisian intellectuals, the most notable among them Sartre and de Beauvoir.

Lilas Station, wants to punch two little holes: *bang*, *bang*! while Melody Nelson dies in a plane crash.

On the tablecloth, I once again draw Cresseveuille from my fading memory. The place stretches from the church to the town hall, a mile or so of country road that the urbanite Gainsbourg covered on his moped. After a curve, he passed the wayside crucifix, an imposing Christ on the cross, tortured by the side of the road. I think of Serge Gainsbourg's obsession with flagellation and death. And of his very personal, infidel's sense of humour: 'If Christ had died on an electric chair, all the little Christians would be wearing a little chair around their necks.'

Once past the crucifix, the republican order of the town hall appears. Cresseveuille, following the example of its bigger neighbours, has built its municipal seat in the shape of a miniature brick cube with white shutters and a slate roof. A doll's house that delighted the buffoon and artist, who was an excellent clown for children when the moment was right. To the right of the building, there is a signpost: 'Road considered Useless.' Going back towards the district road there is a surprise, another signpost: 'The Greenwich Meridian passes through here,' longitude zero.

Jane had bought a house on the time-line delineated from London. She didn't do this intentionally. And because she never does anything intentionally, everything happens. Even the improbable.

A snob, Gonzague Saint Bris refused to be reasonable, as befits a good aristocrat. At the *Castel*, or the *Flore*, he had often crossed paths with the older Pierre Grimblat, filmmaker and publicist. The man with a dazzling smile was born in 1922 into the fragrance of metal dust from the Rue Saint-Maure in Paris, an area of metal workshops before the war. Yesterday, I started reading his memoirs: *Searching for a Young Man Loving Cinema: Memories*. I took it to Deauville. It was thanks to him that happiness arrived. Jane and Serge fell in love during the shooting of his film *Slogan*.

In 1946, Grimblat, a Jew in the Resistance who escaped from German aggression, finds a job in Deauville, where the hotel *Normandy* and the casino emerge from the long winter of the occupation. Dressed in black tie, the smooth talker is charged with enticing clients onto the gambling tables. 'Outside, at low tide, I discover an immense deserted beach still placed, like a reminder of a still-present reality, under the protection of enormous German bunkers,' he writes. 'But these concrete monstrosities have been freshly repainted in cheerful colours. Among others, I remember one of them painted pink, with the inscription: *To the Marquise de Sévigné*, with sweet treats artfully displayed in the battlements. And in the shadows, where cannons and machine guns had been hidden not long before, I glimpse the surprised face of a saleswoman. At twenty, absurdity is a vague notion.' The next year the bunkers are replaced by white bathing huts. The future welcomes the baby-boomers.

Between them, Jane and Serge tie together different stories: like Grimblat, Serge has lived through the war. She hasn't – no more than Gonzague Saint Bris. Jane's is the swinging generation. While Gainsbourg is exploring bunkers, she is selling dreams. This dual entity would have been perfectly understood by the ravers of the AIDS era, who hung out at the Paris club *Palace* in the early 1980s, the '24-hour party people'. Gainsbourg is in his element here. At the same time as I am drinking a last beer, as chilled as Russian vodka, at the *Central*, on 8 August 2017 at half past midnight, Gonzague takes the D 675 towards Cabourg, and smashes his life against a tree. An era comes to an end.

Portrait of Jane Birkin, taken in the Sixties.
(Photo by REPORTERS ASSOCIES/Gamma-Keystone via Getty Images)

two

Jane from London

· ·

*P*ierre Grimblat was, for Jane and Serge, the master of happenstance. He opened up the horizon of possibilities and remained proud of this until his death at 93. Without him, Jane would never have reinvented the French language, nor inspired such masterpieces as the song 'Les Dessous chics' (Chic Underwear). Without doubt she would have done something else, but nothing would have ever been the same. Without this man: no Serge, no Charlotte, no Lou. She knows this well, but all of a sudden, one spring day in 2017, when I am facing her, she once again becomes conscious of that fact.

Jane is 70 and ravishing. In the kitchen of her Paris home, she glances at me above her college-style glasses with a surprised look. Abruptly, she realises the value of that debt. 'But yes, of course,' she exclaims, 'it's enormous!' She is so grateful! And so pained at not having thanked 'Pierre' enough when there was still time to do so, no doubt because 'Serge' took up all the space!

Slogan gave the girl the time that was needed to seduce the love of her life. Grimblat breathed his last in the summer of 2016. It's too late to express gratitude. But the actress can't just swat away lightly what he gave her. She's not forgetful. These two men,

Serge and Pierre, chose her. They didn't reject the naïve teenager: ingenuous, certainly, but also a touch arrogant. Her trainers, her flared jeans, the army jacket she still wears, her knitted roll-necks have established the Jane B. style, the headstrong Englishwoman who wore those little Saint Laurent dresses so well.

She has given an awful, awful lot to Serge Gainsbourg, and finds it difficult to express. The reverse was also true but, most important of all, he would never have attained rock star status without her. Jane Birkin can irritate with her excessive humility. In fact, she is serene. She knows exactly what she has given to Serge, but won't brag about it now: she has always been unperturbed by what she has taken. Her bitch, Dolly, a young English bulldog, is snoring. I feel like putting everything on hold in order to content myself with peaceably following the rising and falling breaths of the dog, with its wrinkled mug and unquestionable faithfulness.

But I need to understand how and why Jane and Serge, separated by a generation, as well as the English Channel, came to meet. Let's go back to the end of winter in 1968. An unusual spring is in the air. Serge Gainsbourg is wearing a purple shirt. He is sulking. His ego has taken a knock. For the film *Slogan*, he was going to be playing opposite the exquisite American model Marisa Berenson. But Pierre Grimblat, a handsome brown-haired man wearing roll-necks and with an imposing mane, prefers an unknown young Englishwoman – who he wants to introduce to him. Gainsbourg broods: this new partner does not measure up to his stature as poet and polygamous seducer.

He is furious, a mess. Brigitte Bardot has dumped him. At his newly-acquired house, in the Rue de Verneuil, he has the walls painted black, the colour of mourning. After '86 days of passion' with the fairest of them all, she'd ditched the lover and kept the husband, the German billionaire Gunter Sachs. Inconsolable, Gainsbourg displays life-size photos of her taken by Sam Lévin, photographer to the stars: showing her by turns lascivious, a sex bomb, a model of physical perfection.

In this disheartened state of mind, Serge, 40 years of age, receives the 'little English girl' – 'Djenne'– who is 21. She's not aware at the time of the talents of the creator of songs such as 'La Javanaise' (The Javanaise). She thinks his name is 'Serge Bourguignon': the only thing she knows of French culture is the eponymous beef dish. No, she didn't confuse him with Serge Bourguignon, an actual director, mostly forgotten today despite receiving an Oscar in 1962, for *Sundays and Cybèle*. She's never heard of that. And, what's more, she doesn't care.

Jane Birkin already has her own style: eyes as blue as the North Sea, the college-girl fringe, the slender body, the impossibly curvaceous backside. She wears little 'pop art' outfits, very tailored frilly silk blouses, and no bra. Her smile reveals a charming diastema, a gap between the front teeth, known as '*dents du bonheur*': in Africa, it is thought that by letting air pass, they give free flow to the elements and thus contribute to fertility.

Aristocratic, elegant, she exudes an explosive sensitivity. One needs to learn to read between her lines, more so now than ever. Everything is important, especially lacunae and little trifles. If Jane had carried a hippie bag made of patchwork and beads, things would have turned out differently. Too sweet. But still, contrast and daring are at the heart of Jane B.

For a long time, she appeared with a covered woven wicker basket. She got it for one or two pounds. She was seventeen, hanging out in the West End of London, in Theatreland, where she came across a Portuguese basket stall. Jane turned this *cestinho* – a little round rustic basket of migrant origins – into a symbol of Bohemian freedom for the jet set. The simple truth is, her basket is large enough for her favourite doll, her keys, her girly stuff, some sandwiches and cuddly toys: she will soon become a mother.

It is from London, of course, that Pierre Grimblat brings us Jane Birkin, in the middle of May '68. He presents the miniskirt-wearing Englishwoman to a perfect specimen of French history: a singer of immigrant parentage, a Russian Jew, ambivalent in his tastes. The romance blossoms at a peculiar time, a crossroads between the old and the new. The 'teenagers' bring in the ubiquitous wearing of jeans, trainers and white T-shirts, à la James Dean. The boys grow their hair long. The girls wear jackets, large belts, they snub the creeps and ride motorbikes. For all that, as Sylvie Vartan sings in 'Comme un garçon' (Just like a Guy) in 1967: in her lover's arms, the girl once again becomes a child, 'lost when you're not here'. It's like we're together and yet the moment has already gone.

In cinemas, Gaullist France waits for the arrival of the usherettes and their wicker baskets, 'sweets, toffees, choc-ices, chocolate', while watching pre-war singers populate the screen advertising space pioneered by companies like 'Jean Mineur, Champs-Élysées, tel. Balzac 0001'. Jane Birkin has discovered this side of France at the age of seventeen, in 1963. A French education is part of the upbringing of British upper-class youth.

Thus, the Birkin parents send their daughter to Paris in order to learn the language of Molière. The endeavour isn't a great success. 'I was,' she says, '*bad spelling*: I wrote everything backwards, I was dyslexic. I was useless at English, useless at French; they kicked me out of school.'

Jane is a girl from a good family. She ticks all the boxes. For her 'debutante's' education, as far as aristocratic balls go, she needs to learn two or three things that will get her married. And since her French doesn't amount to much, Jane learns how to make chocolate truffles. An asset. In Paris, she and other well-to-do English girls stay with the Countess Puget, at 67b, Boulevard Lannes. 'There were six or seven of us, we all spoke English. There were those we were allowed to go out with, as long as they were princes and we went to *Maxim's*. I had two sweet boyfriends myself, one French – who knows, if he's a widower, it would be nice to cross paths with someone who thought you were great at the age of sixteen! – and an English actor, who was my brother's best friend. These two were allowed to take me out in the afternoon. We went punting in the Bois de Boulogne and that was that, we returned to Madame "Poujet".'

There is a lady living on the ground floor at Boulevard Lannes who the young Englishwoman does not know: Édith Piaf. At her death, Jane notices a crowd gathering outside the gate, without understanding why. No doubt Serge Gainsbourg, like other artists, comes to pay homage to the 'Kid Piaf' before her coffin, but Jane knows nothing of this world. In her personal diary, she makes the observation that the wind on those days lifts her skirt, revealing her suspender belt, which annoys her.

She also relates that some onlookers she passes on the Boulevard Lannes whisper: 'Look, look, it's Françoise Hardy'; she's flattered. She does know about Hardy; obviously, since the slender Parisian is at number one in France, with 'Tous les garçons et les filles' (All the Girls and Boys): she has sold more than a million copies of the record and her partner, the photographer Jean-Marie Périer, has elevated her to pop icon status. Jane has bought her EP. Back in London, five months later, she finds the singer photographed across fifteen pages by the American William Klein, for the magazine *Vogue*.

In 1965, the French girls of the elegant sixteenth arrondissement scoffed at badly-dressed English girls. 'They, on the other hand – they were brushed like racehorses, with shiny hair held by a velvet ribbon. They wore earrings and matching necklaces of false pearls – maybe real ones …' Like the Hermès bag that went so well 'with the little burgundy twinset, the midi tartan skirts, chain loafers – they were all the same.'

And when everyone's modelled on the same type, everyone's grey, according to Birkin. So the 'badly dressed', slipping on their stupid high heels 'with slightly cracked varnish', instigate a rebellion. They're still a little embarrassed by their badly-cut denim skirts, and by their jumpers that do everything except match. They had their revenge two years later, with the arrival of stick-thin models like Twiggy, and of Swinging London. The adolescent, androgynous nymphets took to 'bargain basement fashion', dethroning classy, Dior-clad 30 year olds hands down.

Style is now 'British', or it's nothing. Romance belongs to the French. They love – in a visceral sense – love affairs, couples, love at first sight and separations. In 1961, all of France is captivated by the encounter between Johnny Hallyday, idol of the young, and the blonde Sylvie Vartan. The romance is spread by *Salut les copains*, the cult magazine during the glory years of those aged ten to nineteen, whom the sociologist Edgar Morin, writing in *Le Monde*, identified as the '*décagénaires*'; the same Edgar Morin who invented the expression '*yé-yé*',* in 1962, the day after a notorious concert at Place de la Nation. They are good-looking, young and famous. Johnny does his military service, Sylvie goes to see him at the barracks. The war hasn't touched them, whereas it has struck the Ginsburg family** in full force.

Grimblat wants to adapt, for the cinema, a love story that has caused him great distress: a certain Laurence, with whom he commits adultery, has left him, and this is something he obsesses over. The synopsis of *Slogan* is simple: Serge Faberger, a director of advertising films who is about to be given an award in Venice and whose wife (the excellent Andréa Parisy) is pregnant (which – during the film's writing – is in fact the case for Gainsbourg's wife, Françoise Pancrazzi) falls passionately in love with the young Évelyne, an uninhibited Englishwoman.

....

* A style of mid-20th century French pop music; the local answer to the 'British Beat'. *Yé-yé* was much-popularised by Gainsbourg and Françoise Hardy in particular, often via the radio show/magazine *Salut les Copains* (Hello Mateys).

** At birth, Serge was named Lucien by his parents Joseph and Olga Ginsburg. He later took the name 'Serge Gainsbourg', in homage to the painter Thomas Gainsborough.

For the female role, Pierre Grimblat is looking for a 'wild child like Laurence; I look in Paris, nothing, in Rome, nothing, in Madrid, nothing, in Munich, nothing.' To scout London, he asks Just Jaeckin, the future director of *Emmanuelle*, for help. Then he organises a casting 'at the studios of my friend, the director Hugh Hudson, in Chelsea. Burt Bacharach's music was fashionable at the time. We got the girls to enter to the tune of "I'll Never Fall in Love Again",' a song announcing the impending love debacle. The morning is fruitless and Grimblat has to go back to Paris in the evening. This afternoon is his last chance, and a feeling of anguish is building.

The talent scouts break for lunch at *Alvaro's* on the King's Road. 'And there I see a dishevelled girl who was eating with her friend. Stunning. Through the waiter, I send her a little message to invite her to the casting. She responds: "I'm busy at four o'clock." And that's when I know it's her.' Her name is Jane. She's full of herself. She has the unselfconsciousness of youth without being altogether carefree. Divorced from a famous man, the composer John Barry, although Grimblat doesn't know it, she has a baby, Kate. She's accepted an acting role in French when she spoke it so badly! He chose her for her beauty, but also her facetiousness: 'she had these impossibly bent legs and, before her screen test, I snarl at her: "Do you really have to show off legs like that?" She answers: "No, I can get them straightened out if you pay for the operation."' Jane has the one imperfection that girls, from the *in* generation to the *swag* generation, would later envy her for: her slender thighs don't meet in the middle, they leave a gap all the way to the knees. When he finally opened his eyes, Serge found these legs perfect.

Grimblat likes beginners, 'docile instruments'. That's fortuitous. 'Jane had made a two-minute appearance in Antonioni's *Blow-Up*, where she and a little friend romp about in rolls of paper for the requirements of a photo shoot.' Grimblat is being a bit simplistic: *Blow-Up*, a beautiful Antonioni picture, inspired by a labyrinthine Julio Cortázar story, *Las babas del diablo*, is an important film. It is Jane Birkin's big break, critiques of the film point out that it features the 'first appearance of pubic hair in a Western film that is not classified as pornographic.' The Italian director has noticed that London was being swept by a new wind.

In effect, there is a class revolution underway in England. Popular 'accents' from the whole country are now in fashion, obliging even the rigorous BBC to pipe down a bit. Jane is unequivocal: the United Kingdom is being swept up by a gust that still delights her. 'I was in love with the voice of John Barry, who was from the North. The fashion photographers were cockneys, there was a mix of everything. A certain arrogance came with this revolution that we hadn't had before, the conceit of thinking one knew what was what.'

Whilst Jane is skilfully making chocolate truffles, she also fits in with the profusion of creatures of Swinging London, this sparkling London that proclaims its symbols: the models Twiggy and Jean Shrimpton; the photographer David Bailey; the rockers – The Who, The Kinks, The Small Faces, The Rolling Stones – who are broadcast on the pirate radio station

Radio Caroline, which is set up on a ship beyond French or British territorial waters. London inspires a youth that is immersed in pacifist and anti-nuclear movements and professes sexual liberation. They borrow the slogan 'Free Love' from the Austrian psychoanalyst Wilhelm Reich; they get naked and try drugs. Sex and morality no longer mix. Being modern means sleeping around.

It's with her new car in mind, a Mini Cooper 1000, that Mary Quant invents the accessory of this liberation: the mini-skirt. The daughter of Welsh miners, she has benefited from the recent introduction of free art schools. In 1955, she opened a Terence Conran-designed shop on the King's Road. After the miniskirt, Mary Quant launches plastic raincoats, then the 'micro-miniskirt', 'paint box' make-up and hot pants. Laurent Voulzy dedicates a song to her. On the banks of the River Marne where he lives, 'our platonic simpletons', he writes, send romantic kisses; our virtuous youth play 'Telstar' on the guitar, and don't smash anything up.

> But one day / Mary Quant / Caused great mayhem / She cut the skirts / of the most virtuous girls / Her pop-inspired dresses, terribly short / Have caused an earthquake / My life is in disarray / because of a dress-maker / And this minimum has changed my life / I love this mini to the max.

In 1964, the *Daily Mail* publishes a picture of the class of '64: some 50 women 'to watch out for': among them Nico, Marianne

Faithfull, Jane Birkin and Gabrielle Lewis, who has become a photographer and unwavering friend to Jane in the mean time. Six months later, Jane auditions for the musical *Passion Flower Hotel*, with a score by John Barry. 'So did Gabrielle', she relates, but she doesn't get the part and becomes a DJ at the *Pickwick Club*, in the seething West End. Jane marries John Barry, and Gabrielle Lewis the actor Michael Crawford. The new gang appears in the credits of *The Knack ... and How to Get It* by Richard Lester, winner of the Palme d'Or at Cannes in 1965. Two years later, Jane returns to the billboards at the Croisette for a new Palme d'Or winner: *Blow-Up*, by Antonioni.

When she meets Serge Gainsbourg, Birkin is quite lost, just coming out of her disastrous marriage with John Barry. Their daughter Kate in her arms, she'd fled in the night after discovering that her famous husband had run off with one of her friends, two years her junior. 'She was sexy. I immediately thought I couldn't hold a candle to her,' she says, laughing. However, with her outrageously short miniskirts and her long bare legs, Jane is terribly attractive. When Serge Gainsbourg enquires about the young Englishwoman who is going to film with him, he finds out that she used to be married to John Barry. He is impressed, because the composer is enjoying international success, works for the cinema and directs symphonic orchestras. 'I'd shared his life, that played into it,' Jane Birkin laughs.

Who was John Barry, the man with five Oscars? Born 1933, died 2011, he was recruited by the producer of the Terence Young film *Dr No*, starring Sean Connery and Ursula Andress, the first episode in a long series. Barry rearranges the Bond theme composed by Monty Norman before setting a further eleven episodes of the James Bond saga to music, including *From Russia with Love* and *Goldfinger*. The composer goes on to ink the scores for such major films as *Out of Africa*, *Dances with Wolves*, *Midnight Cowboy*, *The Chase*, *The Cotton Club* and the animated film *Madagascar*. Inexorable jazzy tunes, string ensembles for romantic melodies; in the eyes of Gainsbourg, who dreams of film scores and great orchestras, John Barry is a master.

When Jane Birkin falls in love with John Barry, she is underage; she is seventeen and he 30. Who cared back then? She is fragile. Puny as the result of a premature birth, she is pampered, but is sent off to a strict boarding school 'where if you did anything wrong you felt like you were wrecking England.' She is anxious not to disappoint and keen to impress. She's also free. She runs into John Barry in the lift at *Ad Lib*, a nightclub on Leicester Square. Their paths cross again at the casting for *Passion Flower Hotel* – six boarding-school girls on a quest to lose their virginity. For six months, Jane plays the role of Mary Rose at the Prince of Wales Theatre in London. She excels, striding the stage, singing 'I must / I must increase my bust' while sticking out her chest. 'I performed the role of a girl at boarding school who had a flat chest, wanted it to grow and sang about it.'

John Barry falls for her. He's coming out of a divorce, he has two children, one of them with the Swedish babysitter, Ulla Larson. The adolescent is flattered to be chosen over so many others by such a sophisticated and talented man. A romance ensues and they set sail in his white Jaguar, an E-Type. She sprawls on the long bonnet, crawls towards the driver, intoning 'John, I love you John.' Entertaining, Jane brings a sense of gaiety to this big guy, who is prone to melancholy. When he conducts the philharmonic orchestra for *The Chase*, by Arthur Penn, she sees Gustav Mahler.

But the couple settle in to a conventional and unsatisfactory life. The young woman makes sure the scrambled eggs aren't overcooked, sleeps with eyeliner under her pillow since he's pointed out that she has small eyes. She wears braces, he mutters that he gets the impression he's sleeping next to a racehorse. She takes this abuse, and her self-esteem crumbles. She is pregnant, he is fickle. Kate Barry is born on 8 April 1967. Her father is too busy to dwell on this: he's just received two Oscars for *Born Free* by James Hill. Jane is disenchanted. There's a picture from that same year that features in the book *Attachments*, which she put together with Gabrielle Crawford in 2014: 'There, that's the christening of one of Gabrielle's daughters, Lucy. I was the godmother. Kate was screaming, she'd vomited on me. John Barry no longer talked to me, well, in short, it was a nice little English story …'

Then, freshly divorced, the man marries his young lover, Jane Sidney, whom he takes to Hollywood. Jane Birkin is shattered. 'My parents were fantastic,' she told the *Guardian*. 'They didn't say: "we told you so", but: "come home."' Nevertheless, Jane follows her own shining path. Barry makes off, Gainsbourg alights. And with him, a ghost: that of Brigitte Bardot, icon of the happy post-war years, and the sixties. A strange world that Gainsbourg flirts with, and that his new girlfriend will skim.

Brigitte Bardot and her then-husband Gunther Sachs arrive at the Cannes Film Festival in 1967.

(Photo by Gilbert Tourte/Gamma-Rapho via Getty Images)

three

The jet set

···

Vilified, then resuscitated, in the mid-sixties BB incarnates France, land of romance, of sex and kisses. In her heyday, she rides on the wave of the immense success of *Viva Maria!* where the director Louis Malle has brought together two *libertadores* in corsets – her and Jeanne Moreau. What Brigitte Bardot is, first of all, is a liberated body. An incredibly alluring gait, exquisite movement, with 'a teenager's legs and hips', according to Gainsbourg.

In December 1965, she leaves for New York-JFK with 200 kilos of luggage. The Air France Boeing 707 is renamed *Viva Maria!*. Before a crowd of American journalists, the Frenchwoman, '1.67 metres, 53 kilos' alights in 'a Mao cap and honey-coloured velvet Bouquin suit,' as described by Yves Bigot in his biography *Brigitte Bardot, the world's most beautiful and most scandalous woman*. For the film's Broadway opening, 5,000 fans take over the street. She's being questioned. 'What do you think of free love?' – 'When I make love, I don't think.' The *New Yorker*'s headline is: 'Bardot, tomboy in search of pleasure'.

Andy Warhol sees her as one of 'the first truly modern women, able to treat men like sexual objects, to buy them and dispose of them.' She owns up. She's learned her lesson with Vadim,* she relates in *Initiales BB*, her autobiography, published in 1996: "'In France, a man who has mistresses is a Don Juan, a woman who has lovers is a whore" [Vadim had said]. It's as if I'd heard voices. I told myself it was time to finish off ideas like that once and for all. And I was the first to demonstrate that a woman could very well lead a man's life without being a prostitute ...'

France at the beginning of the sixties is a sentimental place. She resonates with Isabelle Aubret and her rendition of 'Deux enfants au soleil' (Two Children in the Sun), a song composed by Jean Ferrat with the successful lyricist Claude Delécluse:

> The sea didn't cease / To roll its pebbles / With dishevelled hair / They looked at each other / In the scent of the pines / Of the sand and the thyme / That imbued the beach [...] / And it was as if everything recommenced / The same innocence made them shiver / Before the marvellous / The miraculous / Voyage of love.

The public feed on *Paris Match*, *France-Soir* or *Jours de France* and delight in the Saturday-night programmes of Maritie and Gilbert Carpentier, the top dogs at Radio Luxembourg, who are then at the Office de Radiodiffusion-Télévision Française (ORTF).

---

* Roger Vadim: Bardot's first husband, a film director who had launched her acting career.

The Carpentiers, a fashionable power couple, were the architects of several careers, notably being responsible for the ascent of Serge Gainsbourg and his access to the youth market. '*A programme by Maritie and Gilbert Carpentier*' becomes all the rage. They organise the end-of-year shows, including the one that reunites Gainsbourg and Bardot, then they turn Serge and Jane into a star couple. To that end, they create an atmosphere of closeness. Even dressed in a silver lamé jacket, Serge goes to the bistro and chews the fat with the cab drivers. With an innocent smile, Jane defuses the unsettling strangeness of her boyfriend, and with the greatest possible simplicity she stages the progression of a love story, without the spectacle of deceit and infidelities.

At this time, love intrigues and tragic destinies fascinate: like that of Soraya, the princess repudiated by the Shah of Iran because of her infertility. She'll set a new record for newspaper headlines – even Princess Diana, the future media icon, won't match her. The English royal family are already at the forefront of the zeitgeist. Queen Elizabeth breaks with convention, receiving the Beatles at Buckingham Palace in 1965, where another drama has kept the world spellbound: the clandestine and passionate affair of her younger sister Princess Margaret with Peter Townsend, aviator and hero of the Second World War – but married, a commoner and her senior by sixteen years!

At the time, a Don Juan is called a playboy. The Italian *dolce vita* spreads out from Rome like a cool wave. Its enthusiasts are good-looking and their names are: Marcello Mastroianni and Anita Ekberg, Helmut Berger and Luchino Visconti. They patronise the bars of the Via Veneto and invent the paparazzi. At Saint-Tropez, the party is in full swing, non-stop. 'All this will be over at the end of the sixties, once everyone has access to holidays, to the Mediterranean, and to tanning,' Rino Barillari, the 'king of the paparazzi' observes, bewildered by modern practices: bodyguards, lasers to block cameras, publicity deals …

In the sixties, the 'jet set', this tribe of bohemians who always have a 'plane at their disposal to go elsewhere, has embraced Brigitte Bardot. Mingling with the crowned heads and their kin are the conductor Herbert von Karajan and his young fashion-model wife, Bianca Jagger and Helmut Berger, cinema's *enfant terrible* and Visconti's lover. There's the Aga Khan, wealthy Imam of the Isma'ili Muslims, and an accomplished sportsman. At the end of the war, the gossip columnist Elsa Maxwell introduced him to Rita Hayworth, whom he marries and, in 1953, divorces.

It's Elsa Maxwell, again, who has organised, in 1957, the grand ball at the hotel *Danieli* in Venice, where the arms dealer Aristotle Onassis is introduced to the singer Maria Callas, a notorious lesbian whom Maxwell had tried in vain to seduce. Onassis thereupon takes his new mistress and compatriot on a trip aboard his 99-metre yacht, the *Christina O*, before leaving her for Jackie Kennedy, the president's widow. In Monaco, Caroline, the daughter of Prince Rainier and the American actress Grace Kelly, grows up in the limelight. Elsa Maxwell asserts her rules: 'A star's career begins when she can hardly put on her blouse and ends when she struggles to put on her skirt.' Coming from a different planet, Jane Birkin will shatter this conformism.

These people make deals. And they enjoy life, in their tribe, going from spot to spot, cultivating a sense of idleness. The ski resort of St Moritz, in the Swiss Grisons, is a haunt of the jet set: in particular the *Cresta* club, where bobsleigh competitions come with trophies that suit the membership, such as a double-breasted jacket with six large gold buttons. The *Cresta* clan has a certain *esprit* and a sense of humour, and they also get together at the *Corviglia Ski Club*: where 150 hand-picked members elect a *Moonlight Queen* every year, inevitably sporty, pretty and universally popular. It is here that Omar Sharif entertains Farah Diba and the Shah of Iran, who was educated at a Swiss boarding school. A go-between was in charge of taking women to the monarch, preferably blondes. He then organised amorous dates at the Teheran *Hilton*, where he showered them with emeralds and sapphires. He received his guests in Switzerland with 'barrels of caviar', according to the excellent documentary *The Jet Set in the Sixties* by Sabine Carbon.

What we now call the 'tabloids' loved these troubled love stories, taking delight in the antics of the *rich and beautiful*. They are well-served in 1966. In late summer, the current affairs programme *Cinq colonnes à la une* – produced on ORTF by the serious professionals Pierre Desgraupes, Pierre Dumayet, Pierre Lazareff and Igor Barrère, accomplished masters of the news – is taken by surprise: Brigitte Bardot has secretly married, in Las Vegas, the German billionaire and playboy Gunter Sachs, heir to the von Opel family. 'The news that the French star of stars, the incarnation of the Gaullist Republic, got married [on 14 July] to a German billionaire, in a ceremony held in English, on American soil, travelling in the private plane of one of the Kennedy brothers, left us all dumbfounded. And the details of the story, set in the golden age of Saint-Tropez, never ceased to make it tremendously romantic and fanciful in the extreme,' writes Henry-Jean Servat in *Paris Match*, in May 2011, on the occasion of the death of Gunter Sachs, who had committed suicide in Gstaad in order to escape Alzheimer's.

The silly tone of *Cinq colonnes à la une* is striking: 'We are happy to exclusively feature the pictures of their wedding. Here they are, as they were on 14 July in Las Vegas. Eight minutes and seven dollars, before a judge in Nevada.' The footage, provided by the gang of '*Pieds Nickelés*' ('Stooges'), a small group of witnesses, sidekicks and exclusive photographers, is mute. 'Pity', says the grave voice of Pierre Desgraupes, who continues: 'There you have it. They say their vows in English ... According to rumour, it was on 7 July that they decided to get married. Doing whatever takes your fancy in just seven days: that's really not bad at all.' She is in a purple dress, he in a navy-blue blazer and white trousers. They drink champagne and smooch. They go to the casino, 'but we'd forgotten to take any money,' Bardot says in a voiceover. 'We hadn't slept in three days, we'd hoodwinked all the journalists, we'd bought plane tickets under false names – I was Madame Mordat, he was Monsieur Schar.' Everything is staged and recorded by Sachs who, according to rumour, had married

Bardot as the result of a bet with friends. She is a hunting trophy.

They travel in secret. Nonetheless, in Los Angeles, a crowd of journalists awaits them. They lie, pretend to be leaving for the *Beverly Hills Hotel*, depart on board Edward Kennedy's jet, festooned with an enormous bouquet of white roses. It's almost a state occasion. 'Madame Gunter Sachs, that's a name that suits her; in fact, all names suit her,' the audibly moved ORTF voice goes on. The programme continues: 'Now you are going to see how relaxing happiness is. "Where do you want to go?" Gunter asks. "To Tahiti", says Brigitte: that very night, life is no longer private. The honeymoon takes place in the air. The most beautiful image of the morning makes you want to go travelling,' it's of the two lovebirds on the plane, discovering Tahiti through the window. Brigitte is playful. They wear the flower necklaces with aplomb.

When Sachs meets BB in Gassin, at the restaurant of his friends Picolette and Lina, he's already made a name for himself on account of his romance with Princess Soraya. As soon as the paths of the German and the woman from Saint-Tropez cross, everything turns into legend. Leaving the restaurant, they go to the *Papagayo*, each in their own Rolls, driving side by side. Their night ends at the famous *La Ponche* hotel. The two lovers see each other every day. We are in the Technicolor era. The mutual passion of the star and the playboy – one year of bliss, a divorce in 1969 – will be filmed from A to Z.

Gunter is not a man of half measures. One evening, he gives her three bracelets in blue, white and red, made of sapphires, diamonds and rubies, and asks her to marry him. In Germany, *Paris Match* has us know, 'she's discovering the family properties where, in the space of two hours, surrounded by Bavarian forests and hunting trophies, which she finds nauseating, tailors make traditional outfits for her to roam the family estate in.' He lives his playboy life, has a thousand roses released from a helicopter above La Madrague, but cheats on her. They live separate lives. In 1967, she leaves to shoot the Serge Bourguignon film *Two Weeks in September* in London and Scotland, with Laurent Terzieff.

Gainsbourg and Sachs share two passions: Brigitte Bardot and painting. A high-roller and a gambler, Gunter is a great collector of contemporary art. He is friends with Arman, César, Salvador Dali and Yves Klein. He is a very early buyer of Italian *arte povera*, of works by Lucio Fontana or Michelangelo Pistoletto. Sachs owns an apartment in St Moritz, in the luxurious tower of the *Palace Hotel*, a temple of pop art for sophisticated playboys. In 2012, after his death, his collection is sold at Sotheby's in London, for €51.2 million, of which €3.7 million (including fees) goes on a Bardot by Warhol.

In 1975, he finally acquires the portrait of his ex-wife that he had himself commissioned from Andy Warhol. The New Yorker takes nearly eight years to produce a series of eight canvases. To paint Bardot, he takes inspiration from a famous photograph of her taken by Richard Avedon in 1959, all open hair and plump lips. He is captivated. Brigitte Bardot is stunning.

What deals a fatal blow to the Bardot-Sachs marriage would appear to be an excess of light. The perpetrator of the impending misfortune is the Cannes Festival. In 1967, the husband wants to present *Batouk*, a film he's produced, at the festival. This very experimental documentary, directed by Jean-Jacques Manigot, deals with Africa, with blackness. The film is intelligent, there is nothing glam about it; it is interspersed with poems by Aimé Césaire and Senghor. It is co-written by the Uruguayan painter Carlos Páez Vilaró. The sixties are the years of decolonisation, of the discovery of pop-exoticism. Indeed, Serge Gainsbourg had already jumped on that bandwagon. A gifted chameleon, he'd borrowed the rhythms and tunes of the Nigerian Babatunde Olatunji and the South African Miriam Makeba to form his album *Gainsbourg Percussions* around the songs 'Couleur café' (Coffee Colour) and 'Pauvre Lola' (Poor Lola), which he livens up with the laughter of France Gall.

It is agreed that the festival will close with *Batouk*, but only if BB is present. She hates Cannes. Furious, she accepts, 'for her husband's sake', according to the source, and arrives wearing black tie with her blonde hair. The atmosphere approaches hysteria. The couple are surrounded by policemen in kepis. It's chaos. Bardot presents an award to Michel Simon, the friend of Serge Gainsbourg for whom he writes, in the summer of 1967, the title song of the film *The Marriage Came Tumbling Down*:

Not to work one's arse off / To know how to share a few tender kisses.

After this performance, Bardot disappears forever from the red carpet.

In 1967, Warhol meets the Sachs couple at the *Gorille*, a Saint-Tropez bar, during a promotional tour for his film *The Chelsea Girls*. Invited to La Madrague, the painter is surprised by a great discrepancy: how can one 'be' Brigitte Bardot at the same time as receiving one's guests with the simplicity of a housewife? She lives in a small house, carouses with this peculiar tribe of appearances and partying, but at a remove.

In fact, Bardot has never been one to cling to the falsehood of a society where one eats only to vomit out of fear of putting on weight, where vacuousness has the value of courage. Bardot is the barefoot woman who runs as she sees fit in this crazy world.

Such is the stature of the woman who will soon be possessed by Gainsbourg. He, the 'maker of minor art', the Jew who finds himself ugly, the *saltimbanque*, will steal this splendour from a filthy-rich German. And she will love him a lot more for it.

Serge and Brigitte Bardot perform *Bonnie and Clyde* on the 'Bardot Show' television programme in 1967

four

Bardot and Gainsbourg

∙∙

*M*en, confides Brigitte Bardot in *Initials BB*, are a complicated subject. They make love to 'Bardot'. Never to her. Her wrist is Bardot's, 'my foot is the foot of Bardot.' Deep down, she is light years away from the Hollywood industry, she doesn't care about Warhol's fifteen minutes of fame. Gainsbourg, that 'combination of idleness, indifference and informality', (according to Bardot), discovers a 'treasure', the key to which 'France hadn't yet found.' He wasn't born with a silver spoon in his mouth. He grasps the essence of the rebellious actress. A musician from a family of Russian and Jewish immigrants, thanks to the example of his pianist father he has known the hardships of freelance work: pounding the pavement at Pigalle, waiting for the evening's assignment.

When do we really look at one another? Which mysterious, magnetic wave inspired Serge Gainsbourg and Brigitte Bardot to take the other's hand under the table one evening in October 1967, 'provoking,' she writes, 'an unending and unbroken bond, a continuous and uncontrollable electric shock'? And yet they'd only met briefly, on the set of Michel Boisrond's *Come Dance with Me!* in 1959. He'd written some songs for her after that, such as 'L'Appareil à sous' (The Slot Machine), or 'Je me donne à qui me plait' (I Give Myself To Whom I Please), with a certain indifference and no particular sparkle.

Gainsbourg is reunited with Bardot in the autumn of 1967, when they work on a New Year's Eve 'Bardot Special', conceived by the Carpentiers for ORTF. He wants to innovate. He goes round to her (marital) home at Avenue Paul-Doumer to pitch some of his compositions to Brigitte. He plays 'Harley Davidson' on the piano. 'I hesitated about singing in front of him. There was something in his way of looking at me that inhibited me. A kind of timid insolence, an expectation, with a fervour of humble superiority, strange contrasts, a mocking gaze in an extremely sad face, a dark humour, tears in his eyes.' Bardot tries to picture herself as a biker. 'But the words stuck in my throat, I sang out of tune, I gurgled these insolent lyrics as if reciting the Lord's Prayer at the moment of Extreme Unction.'

The Dom Pérignon is flowing, the ice broken, more rehearsals follow. They dine, embrace, end the evening at the *Raspoutine*, a Russian cabaret that Serge likes. A bolt of love. From the outset, Gainsbourg takes care of everything: the clothes, the look, the photo shoot with Sam Lévin, where she poses nude in wrapping paper. On 1 November, they create the song 'Comic Strip' for the *Sacha Show*, and then 'Bonnie and Clyde'. Together they recite the onomatopoeia of 'Comic Strip', he dressed up English-dandy style: black suit, Mao collar, she with a brunette wig, in a large cape and black thigh-high boots, a tight-fitting, bright pink outfit in the style of Barbarella, the heroine of the futurist comics she's inspired. They have filmed the music video for 'Bonnie and Clyde' together, 'and it's obvious how much he loves her!', Jane Birkin remarks, five decades later, without jealousy. But who's going to change Bardot?

Brigitte Bardot has had lovers and husbands. First among them: Roger Vadim. When they met, she wasn't even sixteen, he 22. The Bardot parents' efforts in separating the two resulted in a serious suicide attempt by the girl. They gave up when she was eighteen, quite some leniency in a France where majority was set at 21 years. Vadim turned her into a cinematic work of art. Then she married the handsome Jacques Charrier, went crazy for the guitarist Sacha Distel, had a number of love affairs with married men, including Gilbert Bécaud and Jean-Louis Trintignant.

Bardot is in that full, blinding light that the gloomy Gainsbourg is stubbornly seeking but hasn't yet attained. It comes as some surprise to Paris society that in late 1967 she falls in love with him, suitably married to his second wife, Françoise Pancrazzi, also known as 'Béatrice', mother of his children – Natacha and soon Paul, with whom she is still pregnant. That Gainsbourg, with his big ears, was able to seduce this siren, long accustomed to 'good-looking guys', married to the famous German playboy, causes such consternation that the couple enjoy a period of reduced media coverage.

During a night of steamy love, he composes 'Je t'aime … moi non plus' (I Love You … Neither Do I) for her, a concentrated essence of erotic passion. 'Gaingain' and 'Bribri' record it on 10 December 1967, at Studio Barclay in Paris. The musical scores have already been recorded in London. They have to do the vocals. The first session doesn't go well, the singing is cold, emotionless. The next day, it's a different story. They flirt, and the people at the switchboard dim the lights. 'We held each other by the hand, we were about a metre apart. I was a bit embarrassed about mimicking having sex with Serge, about sighing my desires and pleasures in front of the technicians. But, in the end, all I did was to interpret a situation.'

In his book *Piégée la chanson?*, Claude Dejacques, producer and artistic director at Philips, relates: 'I expected them at around 10pm. They barge in from a black taxi and drift, madly in love just like in the song, all the way down the long corridor that leads to the studio. That's already lovely in itself and, once the playback starts, they reconnect to the essence of the mirage in which they float, clothed only in music and words, drunk on each other, so truthful that the recording becomes much more than just a pair of fashionable singers in front of a microphone: it becomes the trace of a moment in eternity.'

A brief eternity that they enjoy, dancing at *Chez Régine*, shrouded by the discretion of the hostess, a faithful friend. On 12 December, lightning strikes Brigitte. *France Dimanche*, which got wind of the affair, runs the headline 'Four minutes and thirty-five seconds of sighs and cries of love'. Hearing of this in Switzerland, Gunter Sachs is beside himself. The very thought that anyone who wanted to could buy, for the sum of 6.50 francs, the living testimony of his dishonour drives him crazy. He rallies some support in Paris and threatens his wife with a global scandal. Fearful, she asks Serge to halt the release of the title. He does so. Bailiffs arrive to seize the master tape. Claude Dejacques has stashed it away – they only manage to confiscate one of the copies. With the consent of Bardot, the original version of 'Je t'aime … moi non plus' is released in 1986, in support of her animal welfare trust. Of course it is too late, the high, angelic, pure voice of Birkin has definitively taken hold of the song.

Once the Gainsbourg scandal is taken care of the German husband reasserts his control. He dispatches his wife to Almeira, in Spain, to film *Shalako* with Sean Connery, a kind of spaghetti western by the Hollywood director Edward Dmytryk. Gunter Sachs has a simple equation in mind: BB + 007 = TNT, an explosive cocktail. The film is a total flop, Brigitte finds the separation from Gainsbourg hard to bear and parties hard. Sure of his charm, Mister Bond awaits in bed, wearing nothing but socks. She kicks him out. And Gainsbourg is crying. He writes 'Initials B.B.' in London:

> All the way up to her thighs / She is booted / And it's like a chalice / For her beauty.

In spring 2017, BB has retired to Saint-Tropez. Her husband, Bernard d'Ormale, tells me over the phone how much she guards her privacy and asks me to send an email. She answers in writing, terse but dominant. Here's what the muse, who has become an elderly lady with very right-wing opinions, tells us in the spring of 2017 about her relationship with Serge. What has Gainsbourg given you? 'The best of himself.' What does Gainsbourg represent for you? Bardot, in her large, round script, which she has scanned: 'He was the equivalent of what Chopin was to George Sand.' What did Jane Birkin give to Serge Gainsbourg? 'Consolation.' Without Bardot, Jane would not have existed in Serge's life. *Ite, missa est* and the credits roll.

It's true: Jane and Serge healed together: they have discovered Venice, India and its palaces. They have drunk champagne, greedily eaten candyfloss of an innocent pink, have conceived Charlotte. Gainsbourg is laughing. He is in love with Jane. Re-emerged from a 'desolate' state of mind where 'he froze as soon as anyone pronounced the name [of BB]. His star has vanished in the way light dissolves,' Yves Salgues writes in *Gainsbourg, or Permanent Provocation*. But soon Vadim upsets the apple cart: he hires both of Lucien Ginsburg's lovers for his film *Don Juan 73* and, what is worse, makes them go to bed with each other.

Serge poses in Andrew Birkin's white Triumph GT6 on a road
trip through the Cotswolds, Oxfordshire in 1969.

(PHOTO: ANDREW BIRKIN).

five

Gainsbourg goes in to fight

∙∙∙

*T*he destinies of Birkin and Gainsbourg will thus cross on a film set. Birkin isn't yet billboard-famous; he, on the other hand, is getting on, one mustn't miss the boat. In the spring of 1968, they have a very public fling, but they also need to build a relationship. Will they have the necessary time to recognise each other in this world where everything keeps accelerating? The slogans that have covered the walls of Paris disappear. *'Don't lose your life by making a living'* is replaced by *'Boursin, Boursin or nothing'*. Georges Pompidou puts advertising on the small screen.

Grimblat is a publicist, and very glamorous. Endowed with a conquering smile, he seduces a multitude of women: princesses, actresses, daughters of press barons, artists, gallerists, troublemakers … He marries five of them, including the Japanese model Kuniko, 'the world's most beautiful woman'. A night owl, he belongs to the *Castel* clique. In 1968, he drives a Ferrari and has just left the advertising group Publicis, even though its boss, Marcel Bleustein-Blanchet, had opened a creative hub, the 'ideas office', especially for him.

Grimblat finds himself at a crossroads of numerous paths, in possession of an impressive curriculum vitae, a thick address book and abundant talents. A writer and journalist, the 'little Jew of the Rue St Maur' (according to his own description) first takes a position at the ORTF, where he hosts a programme on culture and the cinema, *Avant-première*, appreciated by François Truffaut, 'the real gang leader of French cinema'. He is the son of a Polish father and a Viennese mother, both of them Jewish immigrants to France. They keep a shop selling radios, records and electric appliances in the eleventh arrondissement, they change their name to a French-sounding one (from Grünblatt to Grimblat), they do not circumcise their son and let him perch on a chair to sing songs by Charles Trenet, whom he imitates to perfection.

Having joined the Resistance, the young man is arrested in Nice in 1943, lugging around a suitcase full of weapons – he gets caught in the militia's net because he makes a detour in order to ask one of his idols, the singer Georges Ulmer, for an autograph. Sentenced to death, he escapes the worst thanks to the relative clemency of the Italians who control the border areas. Fugitive, he is picked up by a 'Righteous'* in the Allier region of central France. He writes poems, reads them during the liberation in front of the bars of Saint-Germain-des-Prés. Having been given a reference by Raymond Queneau, he joins the French national broadcasting organisation, where he is in charge of ferreting out sampling discs and backing discs from the discotheque of the

---

* A non-Jew who selflessly provided assistance to Jews in Nazi-occupied Europe.

Palais Berlitz. 'There he comes across another skinny intern, Lucien Morisse, the future husband of Dalida* and future boss of the radio station Europe n° 1. Resourceful and creative, Pierre Grimblat loves to talk. He has survived the worst and, whenever an opportunity arises, he takes it.

There are some 'ifs'… If Grimblat hadn't invited Eddie Constantine onto the radio, he wouldn't have filmed *Slogan*, Jane and Serge would not have met. But the hand of fortune places Eddie – Jew from Los Angeles, banished from the United States for opposing McCarthyism – in the path of the Frenchman. Invited on to *Avant-première*, the actor and crooner challenges the host: 'you speak so highly of my films. Why don't you make one?' No sooner said than done. Grimblat toils and hustles. Eddie Constantine gets the main role.

It is again chance that puts Truffaut into the room next door to the newcomer at the *Hotel La Colombe d'Or* in St Paul-de-Vence. The place is legendary: Yves Montand and Simone Signoret met there, Marcel Carné filmed *The Devil's Envoys* there with Arletty, and Fernand Léger has installed a magnificent polychrome ceramic on the terrace … Pierre Grimblat attends the International Festival of Creativity that alternates at the time between Venice and Cannes. "Truf" has come here to tweak *Jules and Jim*. 'He'd suffered a terrible flop with *Shoot the Pianist*. That film was screened at all the beach resorts and his producer, Pierre Braunberger, called every night

---

* Massively successful and famous French/Egyptian singer and actress, and former Miss Egypt.

to say: "Les Sables-d'Olonne, twelve spectators, Le Touquet, six …" Thus, destabilised and sympathetic, "Truf" spent his time giving me advice, it's fair to say that he's the co-author of my first film.' Released in 1961, *Me faire ça à moi* (To Do *This* To Me!) is the story of spies who insert microfilms into cigarettes, starring Bernadette Lafont and Rita Cadillac, a former *Crazy Horse* dancer. The music is by Michel Legrand.

Jane Birkin is fifteen at the time. She's at Upper Chine Boarding School on the Isle of Wight, well before the onset of festival fever there. The boarders are referred to by their room numbers at the school. Hers is 'ninety-nine'.

Cigarettes represent freedom and everyone smokes. Serge has already developed the cult of the *Gitane*, after having ceded to the siren calls of smokes like *Troupes* and *P4* during his military service. Freedom is also the convertible sports car, Triumph or Ford Mustang for lucky sods like Serge Faberger, the hero of the film *Slogan*. American models for the jet set, the Simca 1000 for the small fry. Metal sheets crumple, and, given the absence of airbags, drivers and passengers often leave through the windscreen. The avenues of poplars and plane trees that line the roads constitute a danger, but the ORTF news broadcast that is watched, during an embrace, by Serge and Évelyne/Jane, his partner in *Slogan*, sometimes has good news to announce: 'Only 2,538 dead on the way back at the end of the summer season' – the peak is reached in 1972: 18,000 dead on the roads.

Otherwise, the era is cool. The agents, the producers, the backers and the directors are all recruited from among friends. One can also be a Jack-of-all-trades: thus Grimblat, now a film director, becomes artistic director at the record label Philips, under Jacques Canetti, the founder of the *Trois Baudets* theatre. That's where he is reunited with Serge Gainsbourg, a friend he's met in 1956. Gainsbourg was then pianist at the bar of the casino of the *Touquet-Paris-Plage*, Grimblat was working on several programmes about seaside resorts. 'We started a long series of very late nights at the casino bar, the *Café de la Forêt*. Then I frequently hosted him on my radio show.' As from the mid-sixties, the two men are drinking buddies – *Whisky à Gogo, Castel, Élysée-Matignon …*

In 1966, Grimblat has directed another three feature films. He's just been dumped by a young woman, Laurence, an affair he can't get over. The gang leader – the director of *The 400 Blows* – returns to our story: 'François Truffaut had told me: "The best way to come out of this and to forget the girl is to make a film of it: you will transpose everything onto the protagonists and it will no longer be your story."' Grimblat immediately thinks of Serge Gainsbourg. The singer has been flirting with the cinema ever since an ephemeral appearance, in 1959, in Michel Boisrond's *Come Dance with Me*, with BB in the lead role. Then he appeared in Italian sword-and-sandal productions: *The Revolt of the Slaves, Samson, The Fury of Hercules …* before accumulating fleeting appearances – by turn as pianist, guest of a baron, man who asks for a light, dodgy character, or as himself, singing 'Requiem pour un con' (Requiem for a Twat) with Jean Gabin, for one minute 46 in *Pacha*, by Georges Lautner.

'At that time, bizarrely, we resembled each other physically,' Grimblat explains. 'I had been looking for someone on to whom

I could project this entirely autobiographical story. I wrote this role specifically for Serge, in affection, in rage and boorishness, with harmonies of colour that I created for Serge.' Grimblat goes to work and enlists the American director Melvin Van Peebles* as co-writer. 'I narrate the story in an elliptic manner, because I knew that Serge wasn't loquacious. That taught me to create extremely short dialogues – six words instead of twenty – with lines like: "I hate choosing because I hate renouncing."'

Serge portrays a type very much like himself, the version of Gainsbourg Brigitte Bardot describes to Gilles Verlant in 1991, 'the best and the worst, the yin and the yang, the white and the black. He who was probably the Russian Jewish little prince who dreamt while reading Andersen, Perrault and Grimm, has become, in the face of the tragic reality of life, a touching or loathsome Quasimodo, depending on his, or our states of mind.'

Slogan is considered third-rate. Only André Bercoff, film critic for *L'Express*, accords the film 'the bitter-sweet flavour of a child of pop art and the pill.' With hindsight, the film has been attributed other qualities. It was also, according to the writer and former publicist Frédéric Beigbeder, 'a cult film for advertising, with its parodies, like the opening scene' – a play-boy shaves in a sleeper car and, having run out of his aftershave, 'Balafre', he pulls the alarm, steals a motorbike and smashes up a village shop before an acrobatic return to the sleeper where a beautiful stranger is waiting for him. Everything moves fast

---

*   Director, writer and star of the blaxploitation classic *Sweet Sweetback's Baadasssss Song* (1971).

in *Slogan*. 'There are,' Pierre Grimblat said, '90 sequences in 90 minutes. I was also inspired by my photographer friends, like Helmut Newton and David Bailey.'

There is a critical and amused look at advertising, with its clients, while they're viewing the rushes – whether for a perfume or a camera – hammering home the idea that: 'Once it's edited, this film is going to be great for the product, it will sell to the young.' Advertising is by now massive in scale. For an advertising campaign for Antar fuels, Grimblat had commissioned a life-size assembly kit for a petrol station. It was assembled and reassembled at various sites in France that were totally inaccessible by road: above the Verdon Gorge, suspended in the Vallée Blanche at Chamonix, raised on stilts in the dunes of Hossegor … Shipwrights had to transport its disassembled parts, using enormous trucks. A jazzy ditty provided the slogan: '*Sooner or later you'll find Antar*'.

The car dominated the common imagination as much as the smartphone does today. James Dean had crashed his Porsche 550 Spyder on the Salinas road, dying at the tender age of 24. The novelist Françoise Sagan had narrowly escaped death at the wheel of her Aston Martin DB Mark III, and the painkillers dispensed at the hospital gave her a taste for opiates. With the royalties for *Bonjour tristesse*, published in 1954, she'd bought herself a convertible, a carmine red Jaguar XK120. Then, having moved to the manor house of Breuil, at Équemauville near Honfleur, she lined up assorted Gordini, Ferrari, Maserati, Buick, AC Cobra … In 2015, the short-frame Ferrari 250 GT Spyder California driven by Alain Delon in the sixties while filming Visconti's *The Leopard* was sold at auction for the record sum of €16.3 million … In *Slogan*, Serge and Jane play with speed and danger in a Triumph Spitfire. Gainsbourg didn't even have a driving licence.

Pierre Grimblat is well versed in the etiquette of the 'playboy years', as described by Jacques Dutronc and Claude Lanzmann:

> There are the professional playboys / dressed by Cardin and booted by Carvil / Who drive a Ferrari, at the beach like in town / Who go to Cartier just like they go to Fauchon

– on the Europe n° 1 station, Gainsbourg actually gave a distinctive spoken-word performance of this manifesto song.

This technique of reclaiming and recycling is evident in Grimblat's film. He re-uses his first feature film, *Me faire ça à moi*, projected in 35 millimetres by the unfaithful husband to his wife, who is bed-bound as a result of pregnancy. He slips in his own advertisements for Shell. References to *Un homme et une femme* (A Man and a Woman) by Claude Lelouch add to the romanticism: on the beach of Honfleur, our two lovers – by now in life as well as on the screen – are running, hand in hand. He's in a beige trench coat and red scarf, she's wearing a padded jacket. On their way back, on the Deauville road, they have a car accident which, in this case, does not result in a deadly drama but in a bit of sticking plaster, some Alka-Seltzer and 'separate records' at the hospital for this illegitimate couple – as illegitimate as Serge had been with Bardot.

The singularity of the film is easily explained: we are the live spectators at the blossoming of a passion. Everything overlaps, everything is fiction and everything is real. In front of the camera, Birkin and Gainsbourg exchange meaningful glances. They drive down the Champs-Élysées in a four-litre convertible, criss-cross the canals of Venice in a speedboat, fuck at their hotel. And quarrel. Jane, just as in real life, laughs and cries, bites her lower lip to display her sensuality.

The scene of their encounter is a gag. Serge Faberger has just won a prize, he is happy, almost bouncy. He takes the lift at his hotel, it's jam-packed. From the rear, a squeaking sound can be heard. At each floor, some people get out. Finally, a young woman is revealed, holding a shaggy, unruly pooch in her arms. Sporting a miniskirt and a wicker basket. Everything is said. Nothing happens.

For love to happen, there needs to be an element of chance. In *Slogan*, that's a choreography of boats on canals. A carnation in his lapel, the publicist is married to an American bimbo whom he takes on a wild goose chase around the Venetian islands, because Serge Faberger wants to turn his film into 'a love story à la *chabadabada*', referencing the Claude Lelouch movie. On a vaporetto, Jane/Évelyne embraces her fiancé, Hugh. The boats meet, and so do the eyes. What is visible between the two actors? An intense pleasure, vibrant joy. 'It's rare, this blending-in of one's private life, the freshness of it was captured,' she points out, having already noticed 'the soft mouth and Slavic beauty' of her future companion.

'All this could be ridiculous, but what we are witnessing here is the blossoming of a love story, I find it deeply moving,' Frédéric Beigbeder observes. 'There's that encounter in the lift, then the dinner where they don't talk to each other. Grimblat is filming, they smile, then they stop; it's simple. "You resemble the holidays" he tells her. It's pure.' Jane yields, Grimblat continues filming. If one looks at the details, there are some captivating scenes:

Serge takes a bath, she looks at him, she is naked. He quotes the 18th-century bishop Jacques-Bénigne Bossuet's *Sermon of the wicked rich man*: 'What else is a life of the senses but an alternative movement from desire to disgust and from disgust to desire.' Another example of the recycling technique the film is peppered with: in 1967, Gainsbourg had used this variation of the sermon in his musical *Anna*, filmed with the splendid Anna Karina. Gainsbourg and the actor/director Jean-Claude Brialy hold a chanted dialogue, while Anna runs away from them.

> GAINSBOURG: The soul floating ever uncertain between ardour that is renewed and ardour that abates and ardour that is renewed and ardour that abates …
> BRIALY: Ah! I don't care!
> GAINSBOURG: But in this perpetual movement from desire to disgust and from disgust to desire, one continues to be distracted by the image of an errant liberty. Do you know whom that's by?

Brialy does not know. Neither does Jane/Évelyne, she isn't familiar with French literature yet. For now, Jane is technically embarrassed and naked, and Serge isn't. 'He was actually wearing huge underpants in blue, white and red. He was submerged, at the bottom of the bathtub. So he could see all of me, because I was sitting up, on the edge of the bath. Well, I was nothing, an English girl.' An English girl who cries, and also laughs a lot.

Slogan, or the writing of a passion. In his erotic journal, Grimblat makes a note of 'the kitchen scene'. Serge teaches Jane the art of French cooking. Sporting a scant apron, she asks: 'have you cut the sheep into tiles?' 'Cubes', comes the answer from the polite and cheerful man who teaches her how to peel onions without tears by submerging them in water. 'She has an incredibly loving gaze, she was amazing,' gushes Grimblat. 'It was a very happy shoot with very strong impulses. I was in love with this couple.' To this day, Jane speaks this colourful French, where '*de le*' means '*du*', where '*bravoure*' becomes '*bravure*' and pique is expressed with '*toi t'aimes pas moi ...*'

'Reality mingles with fiction,' Jane explains to me. 'My daughter Kate plays the role of the daughter of Serge Faberger, she cries and he puts her back into her cot. He had just had a son, Paul, I only found out about this much later. He was very much the height of fashion, rich, talented.' She didn't know the full story about his marriages and separations, couldn't guess that James X. Mitchell, who played the role of her fiancé Hugh 'with whom Serge buys a bottle of Nuits St Georges 1954 when I leave him at the airport, and who ends up taking away an LP of *Jules and Jim*, will be the father of my son-in-law, John, the ex husband of Lou, who had Marlow, my grandson.' The story of Jane and Serge is put together like a puzzle.

No other era has brought about such an entanglement between reality and fiction. This required a certain freedom of movement. The filming of *Slogan* is a story in its own right. In May 1968, there's a general strike in France. The labs are closed, as are the suppliers of film and cinematographic equipment. However, Grimblat doesn't want to miss the International Festival of Creativity – which is the key to his script – in Venice that same year. 'Luckily, I have a friend, François Reichenbach, a documentary filmmaker, who always had spare film, because he knew he might have to leave and make a documentary from one day to the next. François comes with me to Venice with his camera. And so it's Reichenbach who films the first segment. I had discreetly positioned myself on the left, with my actors and extras, parallel to the studio. For convenience, Gainsbourg-Faberger, who wins the award in my script, sits down in the place that's assigned to me, in the first row. I am behind him.'

Another twist: against all expectations, Pierre Grimblat actually wins first prize for a Renault advertising campaign produced by Publicis. He is called to the stage, Gainsbourg still sits in his chair. Grimblat pushes him. 'I tell him, "go on". He is terrified. He fears being exposed. Reichenbach films Serge, petrified, receiving the actual award from the hands of the actual mayor, with real photographers, to the cheers of the crowd.'

In fiction, everything spins out of control. *Slogan* is a film about male cowardice, but also about an era, embodied by the eroticized models of the Catherine Harlé agency. Serge Faberger leaves his wife and child, moves into an empty apartment with Évelyne; it's all white, wardrobes everywhere, a record player with a huge round Plexiglas cover, pop art. He introduces his new girlfriend to his friends as: 'Évelyne, the little home wrecker.' He puts on weight, struggles to climb the stairs, doesn't divorce. She cracks up, falls in love with a guy her own age, an Italian speedboat driver in Venice. They dine gloomily, she's wearing curlers. He sulks. She screams, hysterical, in a high-pitched voice. 'You always claim you're 33, but really you're 40.' Then: 'I'm stupid, because I know it's daft to love a man like this, I've left my parents, the world I knew, and now I have nothing at all.'

In its sad truth and disconcerting immediacy, this film marks the beginning of a grand adventure where love and theatrics, the uncompromising desire for fame, and for drugs (alcohol, in this case), sex and rock 'n' roll will fuse with dangerous persistence. *Slogan* has another considerable merit: it contains the first song written (and partly-narrated) by Gainsbourg that was interpreted by Birkin.

> You are vile, you are weak, you are vain / You are old, you
> are void, you are nought / Évelyne, you are cruel, Évelyne,
> you are wrong / Évelyne, you see, you still love me.

Grimblat recalls that Serge had arrived at the studio with some manuscript paper, a dozen notes, some scribbled stuff. 'Curiously, Jane looks at this and figures it out perfectly. Orchestral arrangements are by Jean-Claude Vannier.' This is the dawn of a new life.

Serge and Jane attend the premiere of Pierre Grimblat's *Slogan* in August 1969.

six

The encounter

•••

*E*verything got off to a bad start. The likelihood of a real encounter between Gainsbourg – irritable – and Jane – angelic – is pretty much zero. Once signed up by Grimblat, Jane struggled to get to Paris. May '68 is in full swing, the 'planes no longer take off. When the general strike is over and the streets have calmed down, Gainsbourg – who cares about as much for student revolts as he does for his first *Gitane* – finally bestows some polite attention on the newly-arrived young Englishwoman. 'She was no Lady Chatterley, no more than a Blanche DuBois from *A Streetcar Named Desire*. She inspired no desire in me, none at all,' he confided to Yves Salgues. Editor-in-chief of *Jours de France* at the time, Salgues immediately smells a rat. 'The dialogue between our two protagonists reveals both caustic humour and acerbic non-conformism. It's a pretty spicy conversation.' He'll be proven right in due course.

For the time being, Serge Gainsbourg listens endlessly to 'Je t'aime … moi non plus', a song in the shape of a declaration written for BB, of which they have recorded an unpublished smoky, erotic and intense version. Beauty is a trophy, and

Gainsbourg is devastated by the loss of his star of Saint-Tropez. Following their breakup, he has been in a filthy mood for quite a while. Just arrived in Paris, Jane Birkin tags along to the home of the Ginsburg parents, where Serge has taken refuge during the refurbishment of the house at Rue de Verneuil. 'He was surrounded by his posters of Bardot. He gave an interview and made the journalist listen, at full blast, to the version of "Je t'aime …. moi non plus" he had recorded with Brigitte. I didn't know where to go. I said to myself: "Who on earth is this poseur?"' Poseur, deformed and possibly sadistic. She is ashen-faced. She hates him. The parents have cooked a Russian dinner. They think Jane B. is charming. She finds them friendly.

At the beginning of the sixties, Gainsbourg, composer of the 1958 album *Du chant à la une!…* (Singing the Front Page!), his first, featuring 'Le Poinçonneur des Lilas', seems somewhat dated to the fans of Chuck Berry. Songwriter in demand among the stars of commercial *chanson*, sensing a change in the air, Gainsbourg now joins forces with the *yé-yé*s. He navigates this universe of youthful beauties, giving himself the airs of an elder. 'Poupée de cire, poupée de son' (Doll of Wax, Doll of Sound), written for France Gall, brings him success: the song wins the Eurovision Song Contest in 1965. The next will be for the same singer, the ambiguous 'Les Sucettes' (Lollipops) of 1966.

In 1967, he is approaching 40. He is quite old-school, made rich by his copyrights to his *yé-yé* songs. The teenagers have finally accepted him. He poses with them as doyen on the famous photograph from *Salut les copains*, taken by Jean-Marie Périer in 1966 – Hallyday, Dutronc, Hardy, Gall, etc. (there are

47 of them in all). He wears Carvil boots and tapering black suits. He has short hair, and the gift of the gab. He is the hedonistic, misogynist type. His passion for Bardot is the exception to the rule.

Serge Gainsbourg thinks of love like of the art of calligraphy: letters that have a body, downstrokes and upstrokes. One caresses, one collides. One resists, one strikes, one scratches, one submits, one yields. Gainsbourg is not at ease. He has given up painting, 'an art that's expensive as far as the materials go, and I was fearful of the Bohemian lifestyle, which I considered to be an anachronism,' he reveals in *Carrefour*, a programme broadcast in November 1968 by Radio Télévision Suisse (RTS). 'In contemporary *chanson*, I'm in a peculiar position, I have the reputation of an impostor, I improvise without much commitment. I have a certain reputation for quality. Having a solid standing in entertainment is easy, there is so much mediocrity. But it's better to be the first in a village than the second in a town, to be one-eyed among the blind.'

The Swiss programme, in black and white, is remarkable. It already contains the sprouts of manipulation, while presenting the outlines of sincerity. Gainsbourg quotes Schopenhauer – 'Only cold-blooded animals have venom.' Wearing a tightly-knotted tie, he defines his malaise. 'I've put on the mask of a cynic and I can no longer take it off. My life has hurt and disappointed me and this mask sticks more than ever.' The interviewer, Gilbert Schnyder, points out the singer's natural grating irony. 'I'm not a singer', Gainsbourg quips. 'But an artist, sceptical, lucid and cold. I'm a sponge that doesn't release its water, I'm not generous. As far as that water goes, I absorb it.'

'In your songs,' the interviewer insists, 'the woman is absent, she's leaving, or already gone.' Gainsbourg: 'That's normal. That's an act. Problems with women are complex. If you look at my musical *Anna*, there is nothing sentimentally positive in it. My life has been punctuated by ruptures and failures.' Jane, on the other hand, has no particular ambition after her failed marriage to John Barry. But maybe she dreams, deep down, of a 'sublime love'. And that's just as well: Gainsbourg is a ripe fruit and she will pick it.

How will Birkin and Gainsbourg go about finding common ground? A bit old-fashioned, he takes a nuanced position when it comes to the miniskirt that Jane wears like a banner. As a voyeur and an aesthete, he has nothing against the object as such. But he also exposes himself as a conservative. In 1968, he says on Swiss Radio, just as his convictions are being eroded by Jane: 'The woman of 1967–68 has a problem. In 1930, they had modesty in public, and now the miniskirts hardly cover half their thighs, when they enter a taxi they ride up to the waist, and that …! A young girl in a get-up like that cannot be as rigorous as she ought to be at that age. I have a charming little daughter [Natacha, born in 1964] and I think, for her – I think that this era is dangerous, this liberty …'

And yet – Serge has an eye on England. He has listened to the Beatles, the first time he recorded in London was in 1963, and he has understood that a global movement was born in Liverpool. He wants to be *in*, he wants to be *pop*; he asserts: 'I turned my jacket inside-out when I realised it was lined with mink,' Jane turns up at just the right time. Gainsbourg's cold blood is set racing by the young Englishwoman who studies him with intense, attentive eyes, who dances with him, the shy one. Gainsbourg has charm. He owes his powers of seduction, he confides to the journalist Bruno Bayon, to 'a kind of non-chalance. To movement … [A] notion of movement in space that gives me a certain allure. And also a fleeting rapport … of disdain.' He adds his voice, and absent expression.

Their story speaks volumes about the era's sundry entanglements. A Russian Jew and an Englishwoman find themselves at the centre of typically French influence-peddling, the matrix of which is Egypt. French entertainment is dominated by a clique of talented immigrants: Dalida, Richard Antony, Guy Béart, all born in Cairo, Claude François and Georges Moustaki, from Alexandria … In 1968, the hotshots are the band Aphrodite's Child. Three young Greeks who resemble a southern version of the Beatles, hoping to make it big in the UK charts. Stuck in France with his band after being refused entry by British customs officials, Vangelis, the frontman, concocts a lamento to the tune of 'Canon and Gigue for Three Violins and Basso Continuo in D Major' by Johann Pachelbel, baroque composer of the 17th century, a German from Nuremberg.

An artistic director from the record company Phonogram introduces them to a young *émigré* lyricist, born in London to Russian parents, Boris Bergman, future associate of the singer-songwriter Alain Bashung. To complete the work, Demis Roussos, a Greek from Alexandria, Egypt, another child of

Aphrodite, adds his dragonfly voice to the blend. From this heap of mishaps and improvisations, of mixed nationalities, 'Rain and Tears' emerges: the soundtrack of fallen barricades and the post-revolutionary hangover, which has become an unrivalled internationally-popular slow dance.

Crying in winter rain – that's alright, it passes unnoticed. Crying under the summer sun – that's more complicated, the song says. 'Rain and Tears' was, according to Boris Bergman, 'launched with the paving stones' on 13 May 1968. A bundle of flirtations thrown in, some whirlwind romances, embraces, no doubt, and maybe some weddings. The blend is sweet enough to seduce the French kids. But, in 1968, Gainsbourg has crossed the frontier, he's on the spot, in London.

At London's Fontana studio, he has recorded 'Doctor Jekyll and Monsieur Hyde', then 'Comic Strip' in 1967 and 'Initials B.B.' in May 1968 at the Chapel studios – released jointly on the album *Initials B.B.* in June 1968. 'Coming from there gave me some value in his eyes,' an added value, says Jane with a wry chuckle. Gainsbourg develops an awareness of all things British. Moreover, he will soon offer the bewitched Jane 'Soixante-neuf, année érotique' (Sixty-nine, the Erotic Year), 'one of Gainsbourg's most beautiful songs, in both substance and form, with Herbie Flowers' bass and arrangements by Arthur Greenslade,' as Bertrand Burgalat, musician and head of the pop label Tricatel, points out. 'It's obvious that the spark of their encounter is immediately ignited by this song.' For the moment though, the alchemy hasn't yet worked its magic.

The Paris shoot of *Slogan* starts at the beginning of June, in the apartment of the photographer Peter Knapp, who has just left *Elle* magazine, where he'd been artistic director. Jane Birkin and her daughter Kate stay at the hotel *Esmeralda*, with a view of Notre-Dame. She meets her brother Andrew there by chance. He has worked on Stanley Kubrick's *2001: A Space Odyssey*, and the American director, who intends to make a film about Napoleon, has asked him to do some scouting in Paris. Getting up early, Jane works on her French and learns her lines. She complains to her brother: 'The first evening, she tells me: "This guy is ghastly, he is so selfish, he treats me like shit." The second: "It was even worse today, I'm really upset." The third, she was so emphatic that I said to myself: I smell a rat …'

Gainsbourg wrecks the screen tests, Grimblat fights back. He consoles Jane, who has come to cry on his shoulder, because Serge has paid her no attention. To a tongue-tied Serge, he repeats: 'She's the one.' 'He didn't say *anything*,' Grimblat insists. 'Wrong,' Jane corrects him: 'He twice gave me cues for my responses.' The very first days of a shoot that's scheduled to go on for another seven weeks turn sour. But here we see the first glimmers of the miracle of love. Exasperated, Gainsbourg harasses his partner: '"But how can you accept a role in France when you don't speak a word of French?" And at that, she started to weep. When we get to see the rushes, I say to Grimblat: "not bad, the little English girl …"'

There is a chink in Gainsbourg's armour. He can spot a tragedian when he sees one. The troubled young girl mixes everything up: life, reality, the script. She declares in a shattered voice: 'I have nothing left. I have lost everything. Not even the wild animals will want my flesh.' And Gainsbourg finds her 'fabulous'. Is making women cry what it takes to get attached to them?

In 2017, Jane has had another look at the screen tests of *Slogan*. 'It's excruciating that Grimblat managed to see that I was worth something based on this, and that Serge didn't kill the project! He would have … like some chatelaine, he would have had the right to make a complete fool of me, because the film depended entirely on him alone. It was crazy that I was chosen after these disastrous screen tests in London.' Pierre Grimblat comes up with a ploy. He invites the two actors to dine at *Maxim's*, to clear the air, on the Friday evening. 'And I didn't join them,' obviously, says Grimblat with a malicious smile.

After dinner, Gainsbourg, charmed and charming, takes Jane to *New Jimmy's*, the place run by his friend Régine, who had nurtured his clandestine trysts with Brigitte Bardot. Gainsbourg shows off, he asks her to dance, but only slow dances. When he steps on her feet, Jane figures out that he can't dance. Does she reject him? No, she is 'absolutely delighted', and falls in love with 'his shyness, his clumsiness …' She instinctively knows where the vulnerabilities are hidden.

Gainsbourg takes her out to paint the town red – his town: accomplices from now on, they take refuge at *Raspoutine's*, a Russian nightclub where he's a regular, then in Pigalle, at the cabaret club *Madame Arthur's*. Great moments, Jane tells me, 'with all these men dressed up as women who came to sit on our knees like scampering little cockerels. They all knew each other, because he and his father had worked there as pianists: "Ah, hi Sergio!", they shouted, sending him kisses, while putting feathers in my hair ... '

Thrown into this universe that she was unaware of, Jane ventures a question: 'Why he hadn't asked: "how are you" when we first met, and he answered: "Because I didn't care" ...'

The armour melts. So does Jane's. It thrills her. 'I realised that all the things I had taken for aggressions were nothing more than protection after all, for someone infinitely too sensitive, someone terribly romantic, with a tenderness and sentimentality one would never guess at. One day he said he was a "pretend villain", and that's true ...'

Spontaneous by nature, Jane Birkin understands Lucien Ginsburg and isn't distracted by his superficial appearance. She finds their reciprocal clumsiness charming. That night, she understands the intimate link between the son of Joseph the Russian and the piano, and music. He confesses this when they drink at *Madame Arthur's*. She is as besotted with him as he is taken with her.

The night ends in a hotel room, at the *Hilton*. Our two lovers will come together. But the receptionist commits a terrible faux pas when allocating room number 642 to the notorious seducer: 'The usual, Monsieur Gainsbourg?' Serge loved telling the story, and its aftermath: 'And then nothing happened, I conked out, I was pissed as a fart.' In the morning, Jane has time to go the Champs-Elysées Drugstore to buy 'Yummy Yummy Yummy', a hit blissfully sung by the American group Ohio Express.

> Yummy, yummy, yummy / I got love in my tummy
> and I feel like a-lovin' you / Love, you're such a sweet
> thing, good enough to eat thing / And it's just a-what
> I'm gonna do.

'She made off, then she stuck this EP I really liked at the time between my toes. Five days later, same scenario: *Hilton*, wasted, beddy-byes. She must have asked herself: "But what is this Frenchman all about?" The perfect strategy had been for nothing to happen.'

Once the ice is broken, Serge embarks on Jane's education à la Gainsbourg. He takes her to the grotty neighbourhood of Barbès, to the dingy cinemas that screen reruns of the sword-and-sandal films he had appeared in. 'The people whistled when he played the role of the traitor.' He takes her to *Maxim's*, where Jane is refused entry one night on account of her wicker basket. Gainsbourg flies off the handle – he is fiercely loyal. He protects her and doesn't budge. Jane, with hindsight: 'He was incredibly handsome, sexy, perplexing, Slavic.'

During these first steps, there is an abundance of romantic anecdotes. Serge announces to Jane that he has asked for all the landmarks of Paris to be illuminated at 8pm, as a manifestation of his love. They are lit up, and she believes it. Jane says she wants to go back to London, and suddenly there he is, stuck in his room at the hotel *Esmeralda*: livid, watching as a candle burns itself out for the entire night ... The next day, he sends her a telegram, which he will turn into a song for Catherine Deneuve in 1980, 'Overseas Telegram':

I would like this telegram / To be the loveliest telegram / Of all the telegrams / That you'll ever receive.

He whispers: 'Before I knew you, I drew you.' To begin with, Jane Birkin is dressing the wounds of a young woman abandoned by her inadequate husband, as well as those of her new lover, battered by a marriage to a Russian ex-princess and shattered by Brigitte Bardot. 'It was all about affection. In one year, he was able to heal the wound. I also did it. He found himself ugly, I found him handsome. We patched each other up mutually.'

By an extraordinary about-turn, Serge has replaced his French injuries with a swinging London where he loves the sounds, the shadows and the colours: he knows that this is where tomorrow's music is being created. As for Jane, she shows imagination by remodelling her girly 'made in Carnaby Street' look into Parisian chic.

Hampered by distribution problems, the theatrical release of *Slogan* is delayed to July 1969. In order to launch his film, Grimblat hires a press attaché: Bertrand Tavernier. The future filmmaker produces a very to-the-point marketing slogan: 'Now in cinemas: the couple of the year.' During the opening night, at the Colisée cinema, our two lovebirds are inseparable. A famous photograph sums up the upheaval that hits Serge Gainsbourg.

He's in a coat and striped trousers, English style, she wears an ultra-short black mini dress, completely see-through, revealing her thighs, her underpants, her navel, and her breasts, since she's not wearing a bra (she'll fib: 'it was made transparent by the flashes'). She has Serge on one arm, and her woven wicker basket on the other. With her fringe and her flat chest, the criteria she establishes are a far cry from those of the pin-up.

Between the beginning of filming and the release of *Slogan*, a year has passed. During that time, they have publicly become a couple, and one that has already achieved iconic status. They appear on television, in the papers, photographed happy, cheerfully running on country lanes, the one glued to the other, he in front, she behind, or vice versa. Jane and Serge have already created a way of life, they represent a hope for happiness.

A dinner at Saint-Germain-des-Prés with the crew of *Slogan* has changed the order of things. At a neighbouring table, the director Jacques Deray studies his mate Grimblat's young female recruit. He is looking for a partner for the film he is developing with Romy Schneider, Alain Delon and Maurice Ronet, symbols of the French school of seduction. He invites 'the young Englishwoman who breaks everything' to join the perfectly-beautiful trio that forms a secluded and sensual gathering around the pool of a villa in the Oumède area, in the hills of Ramatuelle. Deray doesn't bother with philosophical considerations. The film's title will be *The Swimming Pool*, since all the action takes place around the pool.

Jane has no memory for dates. A flaw in the eyes of her biographers, but a quality that allows her to accumulate good points, to simultaneously embody the housewife of a certain age and the teenager in Converse trainers.

Conversation with her is always a pleasure. Her bitch Dolly has woken up. She growls, rolls on her back. Jane talks cinema: she doesn't like herself in *The Swimming Pool*, but at the time she didn't listen to anyone. 'I wasn't going to be pushed around, which was my mistake. I wanted to keep my outfits. I was very insistent on being myself, with enormous sunglasses, the fringe, the miniskirt, and yet I would have had a more interesting face without all that make-up, all that decoration on my head. We had to wait for Serge's film *Je t'aime moi non plus* for me to finally have this natural face. And then the films of Jacques Doillon, who made an actress of me, starting with the film *The Prodigal Daughter*, where I manipulate Michel Piccoli. Jacques used me for his characters, like Serge in his lyrics thereafter. But in *Slogan* and *The Swimming Pool*, I had a 1968 look.'

And yet, this resilience is crucial. Deep down, Birkin never let anyone push her around. This is both a political stance and a character trait. A huge popular success, *The Swimming Pool*, ironically, is released a few months before *Slogan*. And Serge is about to become, by necessity, a 'Monsieur Birkin' in the presence of the new rising star of French cinema.

Serge and Jane on the set of Jacques Deray's *The Swimming Pool* in Saint Tropez, August, 1968.

(Photo by Jean-Pierre BONNOTTE/Gamma-Rapho via Getty Images)

seven

The hell of St. Tropez

. . . .

*I*n 1959, Gainsbourg dreamt up a tormented tableau on the album jacket of *Gainsbourg n° 2*: a mixture of cannibalistic mambo and a manifesto against an old-fashioned, stifling notion of love. A jug-eared dandy, he posed in a pin-striped suit. Thuggish, a smoker of *Gitanes*, he propped himself up on an elegant side table adorned with a bunch of red roses and a revolver. In 1966, Gunter Sachs released red roses over La Madrague, Bardot's house, from a helicopter – a commando operation to try and secure nuptials with BB. Two years later, Serge took the revolver to Saint-Tropez and never fired it. Artists sometimes have premonitory visions.

Ordeal at Saint-Tropez! The filming of *The Swimming Pool* turns into a nightmare. Gainsbourg is pole-axed by jealousy. What a year 1968 is! In January, he cries over BB. In May, he meets Jane. In August, he risks the lot. Saint-Tropez features as a rite of passage in the development of the myth, and in the fabrication of the 'couple of the year': so happy, so close, so glam during the preview of their film *Slogan* a few months later. It's a trying ordeal. An unimpressive *pétanque* player, more prone to all-nighters than to associating with the bowlers of the Place des Lices, Serge Gainsbourg is afraid of the unfair competition of two good-looking guys of princely build and fiery eyes.

Hired by Jacques Deray, Jane Birkin will take part in the cinematographic lives of Alain Delon and Maurice Ronet for a few weeks. All of this in Saint-Tropez, the undisputed fiefdom of BB, whose presence still haunts a Serge now reduced to a bundle of nerves. Gainsbourg follows Jane to Saint-Tropez. He carries a gun. He promises to draw it if these notorious womanisers make eyes at 'Djenne'. 'I'll kill the first one who touches her,' he tells Pierre Grimblat.

Gainsbourg, who is caught in the middle, spends the Tropezien summer of 1968 in a state of discomfort. Jane's youth takes hold of life. He is mired in doubt. One evening, the young Englishwoman sees him suddenly pale. 'He'd just seen Bardot enter a restaurant. Furious, he pounces on the piano.' Seized by a complex amorous logic, by vengeance, he plays the first thing that crosses his mind: the theme tune to *James Bond*: composed by John Barry, Jane's ex-husband. Jane feels neither jealous, nor mortified. Once again, she understands that she's dealing with a wounded man 'who, like myself, was going to take time to heal.'

And yet, not everything is all that black. In all her generous frankness, Jane offers her new companion moments of relief, a garden of delights. Observed by photographers, they stroll around in tight jeans, get helpless with laughter. Taken by Mediterranean sensuality, they sit down on hot stone steps and look each other deep in the eyes. Open shirt and miniskirt, they smile at each other. Jane discovers the breadth of the

Gainsbourg sense of humour, but also the sharing of *fougasse* and stuffed vegetables, *Minuty* rosé and olive oil on bread. As far as his singing career goes, Serge is at ease. Of course, the *yé-yé* period has brought him his share of young girls sleeping on his doormat, but the passionate fans, the 'fan-a-tics', in his words, who'll be on his heels once he's become Gainsbarre, spare him for the time being.

The Saint-Tropez episode takes place in the thick of love's 'crystallisation' – a small twig immersed in salt adorns itself with crystals. Gainsbourg is cautious: the emergence of love makes him run away, the process of transforming another being into a precious treasure is intolerable for him. He'd written as much the previous year, in his musical *Anna*: a triangular story where Gainsbourg, Jean-Claude Brialy and Anna Karina play cat and mouse. In one scene, they are drinking beer at Deauville:

> SERGE: I'll tell you one thing: If you lose your lucidity
>   for a single moment, you're screwed.
> BRIALY: Come on! You drink like a fish!
> SERGE: No, really – you're screwed. You lose all the
>   others.
> BRIALY: That's 'crystallisation', as Stendhal puts it.
> ANNA: You're not funny, the two of you, it's the same
>   routine every evening.

Exiled on the shores of the Mediterranean, Lucien the Slav willingly adorns Jane with all of the crystals: freedom, abundance, style, fun, audacity and profligacy. But, on the other hand, the filming of *The Swimming Pool* is a return to the depths of the salt mine.

Gainsbourg knows from experience that film sets have a particularly aphrodisiac quality. For the man in love, all the warning lights turn to red. Unsurprisingly, Delon starts hitting on Birkin, taking her everywhere in the chauffeur-driven black Cadillac Fleetwood provided by the production company. Romy Schneider is amused. Gainsbourg has rented a chauffeur-driven Rolls to pick his sweetheart up every evening in the hills of Ramatuelle. 'I've never found out if the gun was also rented,' quips Grimblat, who had suggested carrying a second revolver in order to defend against possible assault from the skilful seducer Maurice Ronet.

Serge Gainsbourg was certainly energised by the radiance of the *yé-yé*s, particularly thanks to France Gall, the eighteen-year-old 'baby shark', a young thing full of blondness and innocence. But who is he, in comparison to the fascinating pair who are Alain Delon-Romy Schneider? Romy, the 'Sissi'* already famous at nineteen, had arrived at Paris-Orly Airport one day in 1958 from Vienna. She's here to film *Christine*, a Franco-Italian film by Pierre Gaspard-Huit, a remake of *Liebelei* by Max Ophüls, in which her mother, the actress Magda Schneider, had played the main role in 1933.

---

*   *Sissi* (1955), dir. Ernst Marischka, one of the most successful German-language movies ever, a biopic of the eponymous Austrian Empress, wife of Franz Josef. The film introduced international audiences to Schneider, who played the title role.

At the foot of the gangway, Delon awaits her with a bunch of flowers. Yet again, they fight. She was 'stuck up', he 'too handsome, too sleek'. Five years of turbulent passion ensued, closely narrated by a European press fascinated by their beauty. When they break up, in 1963, Romy is holed up in Germany. For *The Swimming Pool*, Delon has insisted on having Romy in the role of his companion, Marianne. In real life, Alain Delon is in the process of separating from his wife, Natalie: he has begun a tumultuous affair with the actress Mireille Darc.

Their cinematic 'reunion' confounds gossip columnists and housewives alike. The script of *The Swimming Pool* brings them together: Jean-Paul (Delon) and Marianne (Romy) are a happy couple. Harry (Maurice Ronet), an ageing but dominant playboy, a big shot in the music industry, turns up to wreak havoc. He arrives at the wheel of his Maserati Ghibli, an absolute object of desire, accompanied by his daughter Pénélope – Jane – who feigns innocence. The eyes are piercing, blue, green, grey. The bodies are perfect. There is much diving and splashing. There is flirting in the blue water. And there is killing, too.

In the sixties, the pool symbolises the fulcrum of eroticism and wealth. But also anticipation and possible disaster – a dive into and disturbance of the smooth blue surface, hidden behind gates and doorways, rows of cacti and palm trees. In 1967, while Jacques Deray is dreaming up the scenario of *The Swimming Pool*, the British painter David Hockney paints *A Bigger Splash* – the iconic canvas from a series dedicated to Californian swimming pools. In 2015, the Italian director Luca Guadagnino draws the parallel: he directs a remake of *The Swimming Pool* and calls it *A Bigger Splash*. This psychological thriller is filmed on the island of Pantelleria, off the southern coast of Sicily, where the light is starker. Dakota Johnson, main actress in the adaptation of the erotic bestseller *Fifty Shades of Grey*, replaces Jane Birkin in the role of Pénélope, minus the freshness and innocence. Nonetheless, vacuity prevails around the edge of the pool with the same implacability.

The Swimming Pool is about moneyed ennui. Delon is depressed. Birkin drags around her startled longing. Ronet has nothing left to gain. Romy gets her senses muddled in a bewildering reality. Halfway through the film, in an atmosphere fraught with suspicion, Pénélope and Jean-Paul transgress the architectural order and rigid setting of the pool by escaping to the beach to swim. They come back late, Jane has her hair full of salt. They have 'messed around': that much is obvious. The realisation appears in the eyes of their partners. In actuality, it breaks Gainsbourg's heart.

A rerun of *The Swimming Pool* on French television, as well as the general fascination that continues to be wielded by the nuances of Romy's gaze, made me want to go to Saint-Tropez, which to my mind was Françoise Sagan's territory. Serge Gainsbourg considered her an unreadable writer. He had refused to set one of her poems to music. He hadn't understood how much Sagan preferred the car accident to deadly boredom.

We are in September: the swarms of gapers have withdrawn, the stars have migrated elsewhere. On the vast beach of Pampelonne, the beauty competition has begun to slacken.

Everything breathes once more: the birds, the plants, the trees – dog figwort, Jupiter's beard, dwarf palm, Stachys maritima. The regulars, permanent residents or natives, regain possession of the place. Tanned all year long, they can gauge at first glance the intensity of the squalls that are announcing themselves on the Mediterranean, or the flight trajectory of the yellow-legged gull. They know the cartography of the reputable beaches and restaurants.

Calmly, I explore the fortifications of the town of Ramatuelle, crucible of either doomed or unconditional love, depending on the glances cast in *The Swimming Pool*. The private lanes of the Oumède neighbourhood lead nowhere. The one-way streets prevent fans of Johnny Hallyday, who died on 5 December 2017, from locating what's left of his 'Mexican hacienda'-style villa, 'la Lorada', which he'd sold in 2000. There is an olive grove, a bowling pitch, a 500-square-metre swimming pool with artificial lagoons and palm-lined islets, a fountain with an arrangement of water lillies and papyrus … Compared to this, the nearby villa that was the setting of *The Swimming Pool* is a mere cottage. Albeit a luxury one.

The Oumède neighbourhood is in a slightly elevated position. The terrain is quite flat. It is reached via the beach road. Everything is devoted to privacy: the yews are meticulously trimmed. A bit further up, the sea and vineyards come into view. I discover the things that cannot be captured on film: the fragrance of thyme and laurel, the perspiration of bodies, the sweet breeze. Jacques Deray suggested them skilfully in the love scenes of his film. In this Tropezian landscape, full of smells and scorched by the sun, the two icons have rediscovered the ardent gestures and rekindled the smiles of their past passions. They touch each other lightly. Between Ronet and Birkin, everything plays out in their glances. Enraptured, stirred, cornered, dangerous. Jane, 21 at the time, finds her place among the stars with natural elegance. Gainsbourg is trapped, he is furious, he drinks and he waits.

I try to imagine the ghostly shape of Gainsbourg at Saint-Tropez, amidst the rugged beauty of Tahiti Beach. Serge loved stories, he loved history. He would definitely have been interested in that of Tahiti and its neighbours. Tahiti 'beach' had been created in 1934, and was then re-established by Félix Palmari – a police officer from Marseilles who was transferred to Saint-Trop' – and his wife, Marie, a winemaker's daughter. Here, the couple buy 'a rabbit hutch inhabited by a Belgian who only wanted to leave, a cart track as its only access, disgusting grapes, neither water nor electricity …' as the owner explained, claiming 'a touch of madness'. A bit further along the beach of Pamplonne, Bernard de Colmont and his wife Marie have bought a cabin. In 1954, Brigitte Bardot and Vadim move there to shoot … *And God Created Woman*. It is so successful, and the paparazzi are so numerous, that the Colmonts start the very chic *Club 55* the following year.

La Voile Rouge opened in 1963, a hot spot for licentious parties, closed in 2000 for public nuisance. And private beaches flourish at Pamplonne: almost five kilometres of sand, an enchanting bay and the vineyards of the Var in the background. Here, as at Deauville, man has won the battle with the swamps and mosquitos. The long, bending reeds that protect against the mistral and the insects have helped that victory along.

Before being overrun by the vapidity of money and pretension, Saint-Tropez and its neighbour Ramatuelle were a paradise. Up-country, in the monstrous traffic jams of the bay of Sainte-Maxime, I was seized by a sense of disillusioned wistfulness. As if a haunting feeling of decadence had invaded the paradise of this club of brazen, sensual women – Sagan, Gréco, Bardot … – who catapulted Saint-Tropez to the apex of locations of liberty.

A few years ago, I went to meet a great admirer of Serge Gainsbourg, Juliette Gréco. The muse of Saint-Germain-des-Prés has built her house along the Escalet road, above the sea, a paradise hidden under the cork oaks, umbrella pines and rosebays. And rocked by cicadas 'who misbehave', Gréco jokes by the swimming pool. According to Gréco, Gainsbourg was of an evangelical innocence. Gainsbourg thought Gréco, who he loved wholeheartedly, shouldn't have straightened the line of her nose. He'd said the same to his daughter Charlotte, who had one day considered plastic surgery. According to Gainsbourg, Gréco was exceptional, because she was so free! She was a human being with, she said, 'all the sweat, blood and tears this entails. And the happiness. I don't reject happiness, it's something I have.'

During their encounter, in 1962, Gainsbourg is so fascinated by her beauty that his glass slips from his hands and shatters on the floor. She's a night owl, she dances. The next day, he sends her a bunch of orchids and a song: 'La Javanaise'. A nocturnal one-on-one: some champagne, a piano, a dance. A scenario that brings to mind the one involving BB in Serge's arms, but this time, Gréco says, what happened is … 'a song, and not just any old song.'

Her freedom is something Gréco has won at Saint-Germain-des-Prés, and at Saint-Trop': summer hangout of the existentialist crowd. Over lunch by the side of her pool, we'd talked about Ramatuelle – which isn't necessarily Saint-Tropez. I remember her intensity: Juliette, who had been the wife of Philippe Lemaire and Michel Piccoli, lover of Darryl Zanuck and Miles Davis, friend of Anne-Marie Cazalis and Françoise Sagan. I also remember the discrete elegance of her husband, Gérard Jouannest, pianist, composer of Jacques Brel's classics, who accompanies her on stage.

'In the days of our youth, we went to eat omelettes at the *Café de l'Ormeau*, on the square at Ramatuelle; the elm is dead now, there's an olive tree in its place today. A lady there made omelettes to die for. Sometimes people have a gift, in her case it was for making omelettes. Françoise Sagan, Jacques Chazot, Bernard Frank* and Brigitte Bardot were there. We had an incredible sense of derision, of happiness, of intense laughter, a total ignorance of money, since we didn't have any – except for Françoise Sagan, who was better off.

'I was lucky in that I had the first Mini Mog in France, a little convertible. Françoise used it, because all friendship gives

---

* Journalist, novelist and critic, a frequent contributor to *Le Monde* among other periodicals.

rise to a bit of sharing. There were my sister's children, my daughter [Laurence], some cousins, all piled up in there, and since the car had neither roof, nor sides, just the floor, we merrily went on our way. One day, we lost Bernard Frank. We had all had a bit to drink, after celebrating something or other at Saint-Tropez – everything was fine, we were all stirring back to life … Bernard was sitting on the back of the car, completely plastered, he fell off, he must have walked back in a … quaternary state to the house we rented at la Fontaine de la Treille, where Françoise did a lot of writing, by the way.'

Gréco lost Bernard Frank and she can't stop laughing about it! Serge is afraid that Jane will slip through his fingers. In this state of trepidation, it is preferable for the son of Joseph, the pianist of the Normandy casinos, to sink into the murmurs of the Channel rather than facing these bouquets of benevolent fragrance, these touches of thyme and savory. I immediately understand that Jane the Englishwoman and Serge the Slav feel more at ease within the triangle of Honfleur-Deauville-Trouville than in the gulf of Saint-Tropez. Of course, we have seen them on the Riviera. But the tenet of nude bodies is a far cry from the aesthetics of a bashful Gainsbourg, who is tortured by the idea of his own hideousness.

I walk on the beach of Pamplonne and wonder if Gainsbourg could have been this tanned old guy, stretched out on a mattress, behind his Ray-Bans. Would he have understood the language of these three German traders in Ralph Lauren jumpers and torn jeans, who have disembarked from a speedboat to eat grilled sea bass? And Jane, could she have become this girl of fine-tuned slenderness who is practicing the art of the serial selfie, while the horizon is bathed in a stormy pink? *Never.*

In the early 1970s, Jane confides in Mireille Dumas,* who asks her: 'Do you like the sea and the Côte d'Azur?' Jane answers with an innocent look, her eyes turned to the sky: she likes old, ugly men. If you put her on a sun-drenched beach, she'll spot what's essential: two white legs sticking out from underneath a parasol that accommodates a coolbox full of hard liquor. So long as the legs aren't too hairy. What a beautiful declaration of love for Serge!

On the Côte, he takes off his shirt and she wears a bikini. But when he poses topless at Cannes or Ramatuelle, he always looks fluffed up. At Dozulé, in the Pays d'Auge, he looks happy. As for Jane, she never played the starlet and doesn't need to go to Saint-Tropez to walk barefoot. And yet, they did go there, surrounded by all the protagonists of contemporary comedy: the night, the clubs, the costumes, the sycophants, the publicity stunts, the provocation. A whole tribe working on the fabrication of celebrity.

A picture of the crazy years of the Birkin-Gainsbourg couple, muses of the Parisian night, soon emerges in the sand. I meet Michel at the port: he moves around on a scooter, otherwise 'it just isn't possible.' Saint-Tropez weaves its ornate alleys between the Mediterranean, the citadel and the Church of

---

* A television broadcaster, who later became known for her confessional interview programme: *Vie privée, vie publique* (Private Life, Public Life).

Our Lady of the Assumption. The gawkers spill out, bumper to bumper, as if Highway no. 7 had lost itself a long time ago, when it still existed, in a splendid cul-de-sac. We sit down in a bar just around the corner from the little fish market and Ivana Trump's house. 'Because *Sénéquier* has become naff,' Michel says. He has a strange profession: he 'connects'. He carries around a very large address book with him, full of private numbers and other information given by 'fixers' and colleagues.

Once the sign is given ('So-and-so is in town'), Michel arranges dinners for his clients. He calls Eddie or Charlebois and takes them to be guests of the Auchan heiress. Or Elton John, Kad Merad, Naomi Campbell, Nagui. Michel doesn't stoop to 'vulgar' reality TV. He has withstood American competition who are obsessed with the schedules of Rihanna or Chris Brown, with their tables at *Nikki Beach* at Pampelonne, at *Club 55* or *La Vague d'Or*, on the beach of la Pinède, private property of the LVMH Group.

'Everything has changed here' Michel says. He went to Eddie Barclay's* famous white parties, but 'as a tourist'. Naked girls and bling aren't really his cup of tea. He would have liked to introduce me to the old lady who's always sitting by the cash desk at the café *Sénéquier*. No doubt she could have talked a lot about Gainsbourgian torments. He rested on his elbows at the back of the café, never drew his revolver. Like any introvert, he

---

* Legendary, much-married music producer and, later, thrower of 'event' parties that titillated the French media. His roster of artists included Jacques Brel, Dalida and Charles Aznavour.

kept it in his pocket and transformed his jealousy into decilitres. He suffered his pain patiently. Followed in the footsteps of Boris Vian, of Sartre and of Beauvoir, who after the war loved to stay at the hotel *La Ponche*, overlooking the old fishing port.

Jane and Serge left for Normandy in order to repair the mesh of their amorous net, torn by Alain Delon's blue gaze. They returned on the occasion of one of their legendary family holidays at Château Volterra, in 1972: three generations of Birkins and Gainsbourgs reunited for a summer break, which ended in the premature departure of the couple – Jane is required to join Brigitte Bardot on the set of Vadim's *Don Juan 73*, Serge following on. The grand house overlooking the bay of Ramatuelle has since become a winery with a shop at its entrance.

The Gainsbarre period: yes, Michel was there. As a young professional, he witnessed the arrival of the champion of the double pastis, who was converted to champagne for a while. A coolbox on wheels, disguised as a suitcase, was carted around by an assistant on set or behind the scenes. Of course we go to the *Cabane Bambou*, at the end of the Route des Terrasses, where, by semantic coincidence, Serge had lunch with his exotic, junkie companion, Bambou. 'The *Cabane Bambou* is a discreet place,' Michel asserts. Which isn't self-evident, because Pamplonne, as he notes, has seen its share of topless sunbathing, 'and the crowd loves the sea', he continues. But in 1967 they also created the 'Anti-beach' there: a club that turned its back on the Mediterranean. The real fanatics considered digging a trench across the dune to the waves.

The *Cabane Bambou* nests among the tall reeds. It's a pretty place with its wooden tables, awnings to protect against the sun, its blues, its whites. 'One could almost be inside Jane's wicker basket,' Michel smiles. In *The Swimming Pool*, the young Pénélope/Jane had placed her basket between Delon, Romy and Ronet. For me, the *Cabane Bambou* is a song by Andrex, king of the Marseille *Alcazar* and friend of Fernandel, who wrote 'Y'a des Zazous' (Here are the Hepcats) and other perceptive songs about French mores before and after the Second World War.

At the beginning of the fifties, colonialism is still going strong. Paul Marinier, lyricist for Andrex, uses the word 'negro' without getting beaten up.

> Me, good negro, black as soot / From head to foot, if you take a look … / Me in French fashion / Because me forced to be, but me not easy / With pantaloons and all this ado / Braces, dickey and shiny shoes / Me like better our kind of use: / All these garments me is happy to lose.

The character in the song ends up dancing at the *Moulin Rouge*: it's a fun place and what's more, it's hot.

When 'À la Cabane Bambou' (At the Bamboo Cabin) becomes a hit in Paris, in 1952, Gainsbourg is still a painter. But his encounter in 1938 with the great singer Fréhel (born Marguerite Boulc'h) has left an impression on him. Misshapen, already a booze hound, having miraculously escaped from an episode of drugs and prostitution in Turkey, the Breton Fréhel has retaken centre stage with the song 'La Java bleue' (Blue Java) and an appearance in the film *Pepé le Moko* by Julien Duvivier. The singer of 'La Coco' (Coke) happens upon Lucien in the street. She notices the medal of academic merit he wears on his shirt and buys him a diabolo grenadine and a strawberry tart in a bistrot.

Public entertainer is a profession like no other. In order to succeed, one has to create one's own legend. Gainsbourg is well aware of this. He doesn't attend the parties of the jet set, but soon settles in with his companion, Jane, to the grand circle of Parisian life, *Chez Régine* or *Castel*, with the masters of the era's television, Maritie and Gilbert Carpentier. Gainsbourg makes every possible effort to keep his place in the kingdom of *les beautiful*. The formula of systematic outbursts comes later, during a confused stumble through a world without Jane. Considerate, Birkin kept quiet. But, in 2017, she adorns the sleeve of her album *Symphonic Gainsbourg* with the photograph of a simple delight – the happy couple running hand in hand along a Normandy road. She wants to free her lover from the burden of Gainsbarre.

Saint-Tropez thus embodies everything Jane and Serge were not. Over lunch at *La Ponche*, I look at the amazing pictures of Mick Jagger and Bianca Perez Morena's wedding in 1971. Nathalie Delon and Keith Richards are their witnesses. A horde of photographers surrounds the soon-to-be-married couple's Rolls-Royce. The mayor is out of his depth. Then there's a small reception at the *Café des Arts*, at the port, with McCartney, Ringo Starr, Eric Clapton, Stephen Stills … At the *Byblos*, where the bride and groom have their suite, the party continues for three days and three nights. Caviar, coke, champagne.

Gainsbourg had wanted the life of a star, but not of this kind. A life in the limelight, but with a certain Slav restraint, with respect for the dead. Without doubt, the Birkin-Gainsbourg couple has invented a unique style: dazzling, abusive, but so very authentic!

Walking through Saint-Tropez today is a matter of roaming through remnants. *Sénéquier* has retained its red triangular tables, its unique signature. Saint-Tropez takes its colours from the sixties: *Sénéquier* red, Barclay white, the master of French *variété* is buried at the marine cemetery under a slab decorated with sculptures of long-playing records – it is he, Eddie Barclay, who imported the microgroove from the United States in 1948. Brigitte Bardot had convinced him to build his villa on a plot at the rear of Pamplonne, towards the Cap Camarat. 'I designed it like a show, or a musical. All on one level, 650 square metres, six rooms, a hundred loudspeakers distributed throughout – and no rules. Everyone lives the way he wants, leaves, comes back and goes out with whom he wants,' Barclay decreed. Given that everything around him was white – the sartorial elegance, the piano, the moustache and, of course, his favourite tipple, the pastis *Berger Blanc* – it was only natural that his party should be just as white. In 1968, as *The Swimming Pool* is being filmed, Gainsbourg has just bought a small house in Paris, and everything there is black.

Gréco shunned these white parties. 'I was invited to them. But one cannot pinch the backside of the wife of the President of the Republic, that's not funny. At that kind of party, people eat, drink and show off. They show their skin, which I detest: I'm always dressed like a nun.'

Back then, one went to Saint-Tropez to gaze at celebrities, these sparkling girls and boys, often fascinating, even in their shyness. Times have changed. Outside the *Sénéquier*, about 50 of us watch an endless yacht reverse into the port. On the bridge, amongst the sailors, a stunted little old man oversees the manoeuvre. His boat is called *88*. Any lamp, any deckchair would cost a worker his monthly salary, or more.

The boat is berthed, 'Mister 88' makes himself comfortable on deck with two friends of the same age. The gawkers stay. The three old men clink glasses. Like those four stars bogged down in the tedium of *The Swimming Pool*, I wonder how to while away the time once lunch is over. It is neither beauty, nor glory, nor even luxury that we are greedily leering at here, it is wealth. I have bought a *tarte tropézienne** at the *Sénéquier*. Delicious; at €2.50 it's a bargain. It affords me some consolation. After all, isn't the story of Jane and Serge one of consolation?

Later in life, during the Gainsbarre period, Serge burned a banknote on live television, but for the wrong reasons: he thought he was paying too much tax. He certainly didn't support Jane in her egalitarian struggles, in her aversion to injustice. He gives more-than-generous tips, takes taxis everywhere, rents Rolls Royces and revolvers …

---

* A famous pastry of Saint-Tropez, brioche filled with custard, which was named by Bardot.

Tax havens hadn't yet enabled the ultra-rich to extend their influence over the world economy. Today, the absurdity of the system is blindingly obvious. On the evening flight from Nice, I read a report in *Les Échos*: the toilets of the impenetrable vaults of the UBS bank in Geneva were blocked. The plumber has discovered a neat packet of €500 bills in the tubes. Ditto in the loos of three nearby restaurants. They break the toilet bowls and dig up €150,000. After a brief enquiry, two Spaniards are identified. The law firm that represents them pays the damage. End of story. A faceless army haunts the banks. The Birkins and the Gainsbourgs loathed vulgarity.

The decline of the cult of the swimming pool began with the Ducruet affair. In August 1996, the husband of Stéphanie de Monaco is filmed frolicking with a Belgian call-girl, Fily Houtteman. In the process, he reveals his sexual prowess and his intimate anatomy, sprawled on the edge of a pool full of blue water, beside a villa in the hinterland of Nice. The 'Rock' is flabbergasted, the video spreads throughout the world.

Of themselves, Jane and Serge would never have given up more than they wanted. Birkin was never spotted going topless, Gainsbourg's intimacy was never photographed without his consent. Their daughter Charlotte never let a paparazzo penetrate the mystery of her chronic shyness. Their image was controlled throughout, including in its trashiest or most inebriated instances.

In 1968, Serge moves to the Rue de Verneuil, in one of the oldest neighbourhoods in Paris, a haven for artists, publishers and intellectuals. He was quite happy to talk about BB. Of his son Paul Ginsburg-Pancrazzi, born at the height of the *Slogan* period, he never said a word.

In Saint-Tropez, Gainsbourg drowns his revolver in pastis, at the bar of the *Sénéquier*. Jane and Serge escaped the tentacles of *The Swimming Pool*. At the end of filming, everything goes back to normal: Jane reassures Serge, Romy returns to fame, Delon goes back to Paris with his companion Mireille Darc, to deal with the Markovic scandal – a murder that involves the world of entertainment, the presidential Pompidou couple, and the secret service. The delay in the release of *Slogan* leaves them a few months to elaborate their style. In Birkin's career, and her passion for Gainsbourg, *Slogan* and *The Swimming Pool* are thus two Russian dolls lodged one inside the other.

Jane and Serge leave the nightclub *New Jimmy's* c 1968.
(PHOTO BY NOA/ROGER VIOLLET/GETTY IMAGES)

eight

The beginning and the end

· ·

*A*fter their baptism of fire at Saint-Tropez, Jane Birkin and Serge Gainsbourg pursue their destiny of being an iconic, vagabond couple. The night belongs to them, nothing gets in their way. He plays the piano well beyond midnight, 'in a bar with the jazzman Joe Turner, four-handed, and then at the *Raspoutine*, with some violinists who follow us all the way to the taxi, playing Sibelius' 'Valse Triste', my favourite tune. I felt light. When we cycled at le Touquet, people shouted "hello Birkin, hello Gainsbourg", and he said: "That's because of my ears and your basket."' In 1969, they leave together for Nepal, the classic destination for hippies, to film André Cayatte's *The Pleasure Pit*. Jane plays the role of a hallucinating wreck, Serge that of an ageing creep with greying hair. In real life, they share the beguiling paradise of Rajasthan's luxury hotels.

'He found it amusing to have this young person around, someone he could mould a bit,' she admits almost 50 years later. Great fashion designers, New Year's at *Maxim's* 'where everyone was older than us! It was like the *Titanic*, Serge said.' Our troublemakers start party-favour fights with the waiters there, paper pellets against party whistles, and then leave with the cutlery, signing autographs on the way out.

Serge is so handsome: a great smile, a mane of bushy hair, some stubble! Photographed with Jane running along a road that's open to the winds, a country road lined with green trees, stretched out in a field, the two of them charming in front of the countless photographers who are waiting for them on their way out of *Maxim's*.

Régine accompanies their romance. She'd taken them under her wing from the beginning. What Jane gives to Serge at the time, Régine says, is the possibility of shedding social constraints. She describes a dinner at her place in 1969. The singer and the nightclub owner were discussing ghosts with André Malraux, then General de Gaulle's minister of culture. They both believed in them. Carmen Tessier, 'the tattletale' of *France-Soir*, a fashionable gossip columnist, suggests organising a dinner at her place. 'Serge asked me if I had any idea who the regulars at my house were. He took no interest in Warren Beatty – but Truman Capote, Marie-Laure de Noailles, Marlene Dietrich, Henry Miller … [That night] I squeezed the minister of culture into my Tuesday literary dinner, with Sagan, Bettina Graziani, Ali Khan's fiancée, who was going to die in a car crash two months before the wedding, Jean Cau, the prefect Louis Dubois and Gainsbourg, who had recently met Jane. There was a joust between Cau and Malraux, on some contentious issues: Stalin, *The Imaginary Museum*, and his dodgy dealings in Asia. Serge watched silently, in awe. The driver, in leather boots and a cap, waited until 6am, an all-time first: Malraux always left on the dot of 10.45!'

Jane pays no attention to who all these people are. What's more, she doesn't care, but she doesn't get bored. 'She was sitting on the floor, with her basket, her doll with a broken arm, who was very important and whom she never left.'

The 'Queen of the Night's' conclusion: Jane never bluffs. She is devoted to Serge, from beginning to end. The couple's love-struck light-heartedness, their beauty, their indifference to criticism, pave the way to their freedom. Jane and Serge seduce like a lover, doubtless because they have transgressed the rules of the era and, without being standard-bearers, have contributed to the liberation of mores and of stereotypes – but with a light touch. 'On all the pictures of that period, they seem so happy and free!' exclaims the elegant pop singer Étienne Daho, who emulated them before taking part in their nocturnal festivities.

The photographer Tony Frank captures the couple's burgeoning romance from the outset. He engages with them as a friend.

He doesn't play the paparazzo in the manner of his fellow celebrity photographer, Daniel Angeli. Tony Frank goes for drinks, goes out on the town, goes to the gym if necessary, gets a tan and listens to the stars. In 1968, the record company Philips commissions him to photograph Gainsbourg for a cover. The young photographer had started out in French *variété*, supplying pictures of Charles Aznavour or Jacqueline Danno to the music magazine *Music-hall*.

Three years after the creation of *Salut les copains* in 1962, Tony Frank joins the merry posse of the *yé-yé*s. He thus becomes a crucial chronicler of Gainsbourg's metamorphoses. In 1985, during rehearsals for the concert at the *Casino de Paris*, he jumps overboard when the Gainsbarre ship hits the rocks.

In the early sixties, he meets Gainsbourg in a club in Rue Sainte-Anne, where he takes pictures of him. 'He was in a doorway with a woman, whom we have never managed to identify. He had jug ears like Philippe Clay, who also sang his songs. Bulging eyes. The first time I really photographed him was at the Théâtre des Capucines, in 1963. He was wearing a suit, playing with a jazz quartet. He pulled little scraps of paper from his pockets, like reminders. Incredible!' In 1968, they reconvene, at Gainsbourg's place in Rue de Verneuil. Jane and he have just got together. The hair has grown, the smile is broader. Tony Frank, fresh from a nightclub, is invited in by Gainsbourg, who hasn't slept either. 'He says to me: "let's go and buy lemons."' On their return, Serge mixes him an extra-strong Bloody Mary, with lemon zest. 'We were both shy. Halfway through my drink, I'm crying and sweating. We go out into the courtyard and, from that photo shoot, we keep five images that we'll use for a number of covers.'

One of the photos shows him with a fag in his mouth, a concentrated gaze, some stubble, he's laughing, leaning on a brick wall in the courtyard of the house in Rue de Verneuil. This was 'his favourite, each of his beloved women [Jane, Charlotte, Bambou] had a print.' Jane and Serge, as a couple, have chosen another one, which they called 'the kiss'. Serge, tenderly leaning over the face of the beloved, the nose he hates, because it's too long, pressed against her eye, gives her a light kiss on the corner of her mouth. She laughs, nestling against his shoulder.

There are countless photos of Jane and Serge. One discovers their sensual side. Embracing, naked or not, never far from orgasm. Compared to them, Yoko Ono and John Lennon posing in pyjamas for a week of 'Bed-in for Peace' in 1969 look like Good Samaritans. And if Ono and Lennon caused some upset by taking pictures of each other naked, recto-verso, for the cover of *Two Virgins* in 1968, they didn't muster an ounce of eroticism. Photography is outside the scope of their abilities.

When I went to Jane's house after the publication of *Attachments*, the book of photos she produced with Gabrielle Crawford, we'd talked about her relationship with photography. 'I loved the sensation of flashes … I was working a lot in the 1960s, the glamour period of *Vogue*, of the Condé Nast Group, with Guy Bourdin and David Bailey. With him, it was often more stressful. As I was often badly dressed, they had to use their imagination. Especially Bourdin. One day, he found my clothes so atrocious, he put me in a suitcase; it was very exciting. He was capricious and radical, but I loved being completely transformed. David Bailey, who was also known to be crude, said: "stick out your tits"; I was horrified, he thought it was fun to shock a sophisticated young girl. I've worked with other star photographers – Cecil Beaton shot me with Serge, Tony Frank. I had studio sessions where I was someone else. Moments of fantastic creativity.'

Years go by and the happiness endures. A short film shot in April 1979 for *L'Invité du jeudi*, on Antenne 2, shows Gainsbourg in a domestic setting. He's just back from Jamaica, where he's recorded *Aux armes et cætera* (To Arms! Etc.). The 'three children', Jane, Kate and Charlotte, are playing cards. After all, his companion could well be his daughter, he points out. Gainsbourg is at home, at the Rue de Verneuil, he's almost obsessive when it comes to tidying up. Jane, he says, 'is a very maternal mother, but she is also their friend. My role is ticking them off.' Self-confident in his paternal role, he adds: 'But when I'm a bit out of it, I play the clown … that's a secret side of me that others don't know about, I play pranks, I pull faces, I put on lipstick. I make the children laugh.' Jane is a mother, a singer, 'but first of all an actress,' Serge adds, watching her leave for a casting in Spain. Of course she's back the next day, because they're never separated, 'except once, for ten days.' At peace with himself, Serge is filmed at a restaurant with Kate and Charlotte, a bohemian father, recommending his daughters the 'rack of lamb for two'.

In February 1969, Jane and Serge are the guests of the programme *Radioscopie*.

'Since when have you known Serge Gainsbourg, Jane?' Jacques Chancel asks. In a thin voice, she responds: 'I think it's been seven months now. Seven, eight months.' 'Isn't that too long?' Chancel teases. An embarrassed little cough: 'No.' The interviewer continues: 'Is this a passing adventure?' 'I hope not', Birkin whispers. 'One never knows, but I hope not.'

And yet, the inevitable is already happening. Their life is in turmoil.

Jane Birkin kept a personal diary up to the death of her daughter Kate. It will be published. It will contain poetry and glamour, of course, but also the bereavements she has suffered: Serge dead of a heart attack on 2 March 1991; the heart of David Birkin, her father, fails a week later, on 8 March, the day after the former's funeral; her nephew Anno Birkin, Andrew's son, dies in a car accident at the age of 21, in November 2001; Judy Campbell, her mother, dies in 2004; and Kate Barry, who throws herself out of a window in December 2013.

'It's such a funny, but such a normal life,' Jane says. 'With Serge, an agitated life,' Régine adds, more precisely. Jane and Serge come home at six in the morning to wake up the children, they go to bed, Jane picks the children up from school at 4.30 in the afternoon, the family eat together and the parents go out again. All sorts of people pass through the Rue de Verneuil, and the night owls add to the couple's peculiarity. The rift that opens up between Jane and Serge soon leads to a separation of bodies, but no more than that.

Bit by bit, Gainsbourg is converted to black glasses and leather jackets. The turmoil increases. 'He wanted to be number one. We were at the *Élysée-Matignon* until four in the morning. Everywhere that one could be seen: the nightclubs, the restaurants. He always said he loved the crowd. People didn't know. We fought a lot in the clubs, with lots of alcohol.' More than anything, he loved being on the covers of magazines and newspapers. He flaunted them, 'put the *Journal du Dimanche* or *Paris Match* on stands, framed them,' Tony Frank says. 'He was the king of publicity.'

With *Aux armes et cætera*, which was to become his greatest success, Gainsbarre has set the suicidal mechanism in motion, and Birkin can't bear it. 'It was my fault Jane left. I was too abusive. I came home completely pissed, I beat her. When she gave me an earful, I didn't like it: two seconds too much and *bam*! … she took it on the chin with me, but later, it became a lasting affection,' he confided in Gilles Verlant. Andrew Birkin recalls the limits Jane has gone to, 'ready to be shaped to some extent by her Pygmalion, but no more. [Serge's] aesthetic requirements sometimes went too far …'

The Birkin/Gainsbourg situation becomes a destructive merry-go-round. Nightclubs and fashionable restaurants every night, with the same audience, 'the same court of night-time jerks,' Kate Barry told Gilles Verlant. 'Jane felt like she was suffocating, like she was witnessing a self-destruction. He didn't understand that Mum couldn't take it any more, she couldn't breathe any more, this was no longer the life of a couple, it was a monologue.' In 1978, the punk rock band Bijou picks up Serge for a mini tour starting in Épernay and stopping at the Théâtre Mogador in Paris. 'He had terrible stage fright,' Tony Frank remembers. 'He hadn't performed on stage in twelve years. He was so frightened that he borrowed the band's merchandise sunglasses – one could read "Bijou" on the temples.' The band covered one of Gainsbourg's songs, 'Les Papillons noirs', (Black Butterflies) that had been performed in 1966 by Michèle Arnaud:

At night, all sorrows get tipsy / With all our heart we wish / The black butterflies / To leave forever.

Gainsbourg discovers that he's a cult, loved by the kids who, to his great surprise, know 'La Javanaise' by heart. He hadn't been selling well: none of his albums, despite their being vibrant works after he met Jane, have been a commercial success. But, with her, he has kept in the headlines for ten years running, he has created a persona that's comfortable on the margins. 'It's not me that's roaring,' he says with bravado, 'it's the venues.' He has all it takes to enchant the world of rock.

'He now begins to create Gainsbarre, who will devour him, encouraged by the record company and his entourage. It's not Jane's fault, she went through a lot,' the French musician Bertrand Burgalat explains wistfully. Jane throws in the towel for good in 1980, having shared with him 'the twelve most beautiful years of his life.' She takes refuge with Kate and Charlotte at the hotel *Royal Monceau*. He looks terrible, she's crying, the girls want to know if papa is coming for dinner. It's depressing. Birkin has forgiven him since. He was fifteen years older than her, the young loved him. 'The kids loved the python skin jacket, I didn't. He had a Rolls, he didn't know how to drive, he used it as an ashtray. He was them, the adolescents.' She was already, in a sense, too old for that.

Jane Birkin was at times 'hysterical', she says – one day kicking her lover's briefcase because she thought he'd gone off with a flight attendant. 'He kept it at Rue de Verneuil all his life.' He carried the thing around wherever he went. In 1987, he shoots a documentary at the request of the *Printemps de Bourges* film festival: *Springtime in Bourges*, with President Mitterrand as guest star. Behind the scenes, where he interviews Ray Charles or Jerry Lee Lewis, he brandishes the ruined briefcase like a trophy.

'Later, at *Castel*, I threw a lemon cake in his face.' He had spilled the contents of her eternal basket on the floor, doll included, in front of everyone. 'To piss me off.' The cake goes flying, right in the face. Serge gets to his feet, 'pieces of dough fall on his shoes.' She runs away, having committed 'the abominable'. He walks toward Rue de Verneuil. She runs faster than him, to the bank of the Seine. She takes the little staircase and jumps into the water. He holds out his hand to her from the bank. Jane's short Saint Laurent dress is pulled up some more. They leave arm in arm. Jane comments: 'There's a mighty current in the Seine.' She thinks she remembers him taking the time to remove his watch from his wrist, a Breitling.

On 9 November 1979, at midnight, he is invited on to the programme *Do You Have a Light?* on the Europe n° 1 channel. 'I've just learned a serious lesson [...] At 52 years, I am going through my first heartbreak. And I know that it's just as violent, if not more so, than as if I were twenty. If some of my listeners take me for a cynic, they should know that I have been crying hot tears for months, real tears [...] I have never been as unhappy as I am today.'

After their separation, Serge sets up a projector, angled vertically, at the Rue de Verneuil. From his bed, he watches *Slogan* on the ceiling.

Jane talks. She is funny, as Serge was, 'infinitely funny', she insists. Dolly is awake. It seems like she's hungry. Dogs, unlike people, are straightforward. I thought that Jane had left Serge because he had become unbearable. That's not the whole truth. 'A separation,' she says, 'is always an accumulation of things, like the history of countries. Everything depends on who came first, it isn't fair. When nothing worked with Serge any more, I felt like an African country. One inflicts pain, everything is too late. One is ghastly. I've written a song that went: *We've kept a strict distance in order not to cry*. As we used to do with our parents, in order not to hear them say: "you'll see, you'll see, he'll make you cry."'

John Barry went off with a friend of Jane's, the latter has left Serge when she meets Jacques Doillon. 'I left for a second, fierce, adolescence. But he wanted us to become a myth, that's how he wanted it. There'd been other people before, and things had started to get murky before. Without doubt, I had a sort of second adolescence. Serge took me when I knew nothing, I was twenty and he taught me everything. He was a father, an educator, an enhancer, everything. When I left him, he shouted: "I'll make a nobody of you." As far as he was concerned, he had made me. But I was something else, he didn't understand that, I no longer wanted to be a doll, he didn't understand. In one of his songs, "La Dépression" [Depression], he said: "You have everything, the children, a house, you, me." That wasn't my point of view. Later on, he went through a real depression, which resulted in some masterpieces, such as "Les Dessous chics".'

'Did I give others their independence?' Jane asks herself, as she prepares to go to the brasserie opposite, a nice place with a sunny terrace and local wines. Dolly doesn't need a leash, she follows unfailingly. 'No, even with Jacques. If I wanted to sleep in the dark, we slept in the dark. I didn't think I was like that. This means that one must always question oneself, nothing is black and white.' Dolly has a white coat with black and brown patches. She is cheeky, she roams around between the other clients, stays in the shade and suns herself, she's free, while Jane, who has just edited the album *Gainsbourg: le symphonique*, explains to a journalist from *Nice-Matin* how important it is to support Serge.

Serge, the Jew, had worn the yellow star with bravado; if he could have, he would have enlarged it up to his neck and painted it fluorescent. The cool dandy had affected a marble posture while rekindling his love for *Gitanes* and cocktails. The eyesore had won the fairest of them all, BB. Jane didn't have an ounce of competitiveness. That saved her.

Jane, Serge and their newborn daughter, Charlotte, at Birkin's home in Cheyne Row, London, August 1971.

nine

The family

....

'*I* gave him a family,' mulls Jane Birkin today, 'there's no doubt I liked that more than he did.' This role is very important to her. Their liaison: a delightful alliance between a 'French-educated Russian and an Englishwoman, which makes a kind of Bloody Mary with plenty of vodka,' in Gainsbourg parlance. The Bloody Mary, a refined cocktail whose sorceress name might be inherited from the Catholic Queen Mary Tudor, may have been invented at *Harry's Bar*, in Paris, in 1921. But at this alcohol content, certitude turns into doubt. Another legend has the Bloody Mary see the light of day at the *Ritz*. According to other sources, it's New York's *Waldorf Astoria*. Tomato juice, lemon juice, the quintessentially English Worcestershire sauce, Mexican Tabasco, Ashkenazi Jewish horseradish, colonial piri piri … Ernest Hemingway was very fond of it. The American writer, after his return to Paris at the end of the Second World War, married the American journalist Mary Welsh. A jealous woman, she sniffed out the smell of alcohol on her husband's breath; exasperated, the latter, it is claimed, asked the barman of the *Ritz* to create a cocktail that hid the smell of alcohol in order not to be caught out by that *Bloody Mary*.

Gainsbourg admired Hemingway for his oeuvre, for his reckless courage, but also because his name was inscribed in all the bars he'd visited all over the world. And that really made Gainsbourg – who'd become Gainsborough for Jane, before disintegrating as Gainsbarre – go green with envy. At the *Musée Grévin*, his wax effigy has a drink with that of Ernest.

Like Tony Frank, Jane's older brother Andrew photographed the family's fun and games at the house in Normandy, in Paris: children's games, cuddling the dog, jokes and hoaxes. 'Jane Birkin has told this story very well in her films. That's where I find the real Serge – a man who loved his family, a charming and kind man. I don't really buy the invention of Gainsbarre,' the Australian singer and fan Mick Harvey, who cofounded The Bad Seeds with Nick Cave, and collaborated with PJ Harvey, points out. Mick Harvey has dedicated two albums, *Intoxicated Man* and *Delirium Tremens*, to Gainsbourg.

Serge and Jane is also the successful marriage of two tribes. It results in a reconstituted family, with Jane Birkin as head of the clan: Kate, daughter of John Barry, born in 1967, died in 2013, who loves Gainsbourg like a father and lugs around terrible despair; Charlotte, daughter of Serge, born in London in 1971, a tomboy who became a woman of exemplary discretion concerning her private life, and who, according to the family friend, Régine, is 'exceptionally intelligent and has succeeded in forming an amazing couple with Yvan Attal' since 1991. Jane has no trouble accepting the satellites who are Serge Gainsbourg's two sisters, and Lulu, Serge and Bambou's son, who was born in 1986. Gainsbourg had two children from a previous marriage, but he doesn't include them in his family unit.

Two families caught up in the upheavals of history, two families of artists united. The Ginsburgs are uprooted. Wars and pogroms, lost or burned archives deprive them of evidence supporting their identity. The father, Joseph, a pianist, was apparently born in Kharkov, Ukraine, in 1896; Olga in Feodossia, in Crimea. The paternal grandfather, a teacher, is thought to have left Mariupol in the Ukraine, in 1904: for Belarus, then England, to escape the Russo-Japanese War.

We then find Joseph studying the piano at the conservatory of Feodossia, where he meets Olga Besman, an opera singer, mezzo-soprano and perhaps nurse. They get married at the synagogue in 1918, the year of the assassination of Tsar Nicolas II. In order to escape being drafted into General Wrangel's White Army, the couple flees. They cross the dangerous Black Sea, reach Istanbul, pass themselves off as Turks. He teaches classical music and becomes a bar pianist. Olga and Joseph reach Marseille, before arriving in Paris in 1921. Their names are false and so are their papers. Everything becomes provisional. How to untangle such a troubled family saga? Lucien writes his name with a z instead of the s. Is he any better at mastering the situation? Even the name Ginsburg is questionable.

The Ginsburg family remains very Russian. 'The mother sings Gypsy songs and fights with her husband in Russian, sometimes in very crude language,' relates Élisabeth Levitzky, first wife of Serge, daughter of aristocratic orthodox anti-Semites, and thus unpopular with the Ginsburgs. 'Serge tells me that, in order to placate his mother, he tells her [that he does what he does] in a spirit of vengeance: "I, an ugly little Jew, bang the most prestigious descendants of the pogromists of old. That makes her howl with laughter."' The family is not religious, but has held onto some Hebrew rituals, such as circumcision. They celebrate Easter with a stuffed carp, never eat cheese and ham from the same plate, but don't go to synagogue. Post-war France doesn't exactly get on with its own history, but still it doesn't admit to its anti-Semitism. A wry tone, sneering: 'it's quite commonplace that Lulu doesn't dare to take a seat by himself in certain cafes. He waits for me on the pavement, and I have to enter first in order to make sure there is no one there. And, when he joins me, we choose a table in the rear. That's not excessive paranoia: his nose really does mark him out for mockery,' Élisabeth Levitzky writes in *Lise et Lulu*.

The Birkin family tree is as neat as Serge's is blurred. This doesn't preclude eccentricities or outright madness. Jane Birkin is the daughter of the famous English actress, Judy Campbell, and of David Birkin. This beloved father, a former commander in the Royal Navy, was in charge of retrieving English airmen and resistance fighters from the coast of Brittany in order to take them back to Britain during the Second World War. 'For Serge, who had been forced to run away and hide in the Limousin because he was Jewish, my father was a liberator,' Jane relates. 'He had also seduced my mother, who was very beautiful with her black hair. She used to pick us up from school, my sister and me, in her mauve convertible. Serge found all that exotic, even though, as a child, he had accompanied his father to all the English holiday spots in France: Le Touquet, Cabourg, Trouville, Dinard, Arcachon … I expected his parents not to like me because I wasn't Jewish, but there was none of that.'

Jane repeatedly points out that she loves the family. The Ginsburgs are welcoming. 'The person I saw every Sunday, because she lived with Serge's parents, was Jacqueline, she was more a part of my life than Liliane, Serge's twin sister, who lived in Morocco. When Serge's father died, when Serge's mother died, it was Jacqueline who called.' Liliane has since returned to Paris, where she has joined her children. 'She found herself isolated over there. Now that she lives in Paris, it's more cheerful; she's incredibly kind, like Serge's father, she doesn't have Serge's cruel side. It's as if he had taken all the sarcasm, while keeping the romanticism. She's like Madame Bovary. She's charming, when I see her now, she's as bright as Jacqueline, the two sisters are terrifying at Scrabble. They are funny and clever.' Jane Birkin once more feels ignorant vis-à-vis this 'family of super brains. All of them are piano players. Jacqueline could have been a professional pianist, so could Liliane. They are well-versed in literature, in music, in painting. They were educated to respect the arts.'

And then, changing her tone with ease, she laughs, remembers the painting Serge gave her at the beginning of their relationship: 'He gave me one half of a painting he'd broken over his wife's head.' A funny guy, this Lucien, funny family, the Ginsburgs.

Of his daughter Charlotte, Gainsbourg said before his death that she was a cocktail made of 'Ruski and British blood.' He

had 'married' a *goy*: Jane. Judaism intrigues Charlotte, especially as the Ginsburg family spoke of the German occupation
as if it were an adventure, a game where one had to escape
the Germans in order to avoid disaster. Serge was very anti-
religious, but wearing the yellow star during the war, the 'filth
of the militias' and the ease with which he thought the Jews
had let themselves be gobbled up, had profoundly marked him.
He gave his daughter a Star of David he had inherited from
his mother, Olga.

At the death of the latter, Charlotte feels irresistibly drawn
to Judaism. She goes to synagogue, celebrates Yom Kippur
and refrains from wearing trousers, she reveals in *Télérama*.
'I bought phonetic prayer books. I didn't believe in God, but
I wanted rules. I was even "adopted" by a family I celebrated
Jewish holidays with. I was looking for an identity. I wished to
belong to that universe that didn't want me. I heard people say:
"You will never be Jewish."' Her father's death marks the end
of her religious period. When he is on his deathbed, the young
girl puts Olga's star around his neck and takes the one he wore.
It's the end of her crisis of mysticism. 'Today, I am at ease with
my double affiliation, between Anglican England and Eastern
Europe's Judaism. I'm happy not to disentangle anything and
to pass this confusion on to my children.'

Gainsbourg has been fascinated by aristocrats for a long
time: he has already married two of them, Élisabeth Levitzky
and Françoise Pancrazzi. In this saga, the Birkins find their
place logically and naturally. The father, David, is aristocratic
through his mother, who is related to the dukes of Bedford,

and military through his father, a hussar in the British army. In 1940, David, a member of the Royal Navy, becomes an officer in the 15th flotilla Motor Gun Boats of Dartmouth. In 1943, he serves with the 'Shelburne' network, set up by the Intelligence Service. The following year, the inhabitants of the town of Plouha, in the Côtes-d'Armor, are in charge of retrieving the allied airmen who crashed on French soil. The beach called 'Bonaparte', by the cove of Cochat, serves as a meeting point. Lieutenant-commander Birkin steers the boats; their engines must be switched off – the Germans are so close that one can see the glow of their cigarettes. The French and English members of the *résistance* are disembarked and the British airmen are collected. Jane Birkin has bought a house in 'le Finistère', a name she uses for all of Brittany.

Jane Birkin's mother, Judy Campbell, is the daughter of an actress and of a playwright. She goes on stage at London's Comedy Theatre to appear in a musical, *New Faces*. Hired for a Dorothy Parker monologue, she is asked to sing a ritornello: 'A Nightingale Sang in Berkeley Square'. Her recitative artistry, her voice that reverberates under the German bombs, make an impression. Noël Coward, actor, playwright, singer, director, hero of the English art scene from the twenties until his death in 1973, hears her sing. Judy Campbell becomes his fetish actress. A star posture, dark glasses, she marries David in 1943. First, they have a son, Andrew, then Jane and Linda.

In his adolescence, Andrew becomes a boarder at Harrow. Then Jane and her sister are sent to a private establishment on the Isle of Wight. 'The penal colony.' That's where they experience nostalgia, doom and gloom. When Jane and Gainsbourg's paths cross, her parents, who love France – where they have sent their daughter in 1963 to study French for five months – are thrilled: their daughter has met someone who loves her as much as she loves him. Serge, she observes, loves her father, David, in a 'Jewish-Russian' way. With Andrew, he shares a sense of humour.

With the Birkins, Serge Gainsbourg finds the peace he had been deprived of by the rigour and severity of Joseph, his violently choleric father. Prematurely exposed to need as a child, he has cultivated the art of being a contrarian. His father wanted him to be a concert musician. He became a painter. Joseph considered *chanson* to be a minor art form. He became a singer.

David Birkin laughs a lot with Serge, who adores him. 'During that time, my mother, who was working with Noël Coward, could pursue her career as an actress. I took all that very lightly.' Charlotte Gainsbourg is born in 1971, in London. Every Christmas, Serge, Jane, Kate and Charlotte disembark at Victoria Station. Serge brings his favourite turkey, stuffed with truffles. The parents-in-law pick at it discreetly, 'thinking that it's rotten'. By now a cult in France, the couple are unknown in England and 'everything went very well for Serge for a week, then he started to worry, he had to go back to Paris in order to be loved once more.' And to recommence the habitual round of clubs, restaurants and mischief. Jane and Serge: like an exchange of exoticisms.

The Birkins' universe is characterised by humour and a very British sense of the absurd, as Jane demonstrated in the film she directed where Michel Piccoli plays the role of the father. He loses his mind, knocks his head, Jane stitches him up. We learn that the dead aunt carries on thanks to the deep freeze. The grandmother (Annie Girardot) locks herself in a cupboard because she is scared of the Belgians, she hates shrimps 'because they had dredged up a German full of shrimps. Had it been an Englishman ...', she would have eaten them by the potful. The mother (Geraldine Chaplin) almost left the father for a Greek ship-owner by the name of Syros ... All through *Boxes*, Jane Birkin questions her role as mother, surrounded by her three daughters (Lou playing the role of Charlotte), her three husbands: Barry who disappears, Gainsbourg who weakens her, Doillon who cheats on her. 'I only know immediate feelings,' Jane explains.

Gainsbourg told jokes: 'Who sank the Titanic? Yet another Jew: *Iceberg*' or 'Had I been a Nazi, I would have wanted to be Eichmann, because while committing suicide I could have said: "At least that's one less Jew."' In 1975, he wrote *Rock Around the Bunker*, an entire album dealing with the devastations of Nazism and the dangers of totalitarianism – some see a broadside against Gunter Sachs in it. There are some great lyrics, for example in 'Nazi Rock', evoking the Night of the Long Knives of 1934. Later on, an unpublished work is found: 'The Silence of the Pope', which denounces the anti-Semitism of Pius XII. Initially listed as one of the tracks on *Rock Around the Bunker*, it was not recorded, because Gainsbourg let it go. At the time, he remarked to the magazine *Vingt Ans*: 'Oh! I said to myself that there was no point in stirring up all that stuff!' The creators of his complete lyrics, *L'Intégrale et cætera*, which came out in 2010, have traced the manuscript as far as his record company, Philips: lost.

Gainsbourg was an atheist, but he 'gave money to Israel', according to Bruno Bayon, the writer and long-standing critic at *Libération*. When he released the ironic *Rock Around the Bunker*, the Jewish community didn't appreciate it. 'One couldn't talk about the Shoah in these caustic terms.' Gainsbourg was often mocking. 'After rendering "La Marseillaise" in reggae style, he'd bought the original score by Rouget de Lisle. When he talked about it, he amused himself with quite explicit gestures: one movement gliding over imaginary Hassidic curls, a finger wandering over his nose, both hands ending up in his pockets.'

There were exciting and funny moments, like this visit with Jane to the synagogue in Venice, as related by Régine: 'We were in Venice with Jane and my husband. We stayed at the Cipriani, they at the Gritti. He says: "I'll take you to the synagogue." It was six in the evening, it was magic. "The Jewish tradesmen lived here", he told me. "And the Jews were moved to a ghetto." We walk through some arcades, the rain stops, we arrive on a square: "You see, that's where they took them." There was a fountain in the middle, we started to weep. "Look how beautiful and sad it is." We ring the bell at the synagogue, the rabbi, sticking out his head, says it's closed; and the head of that rabbi, his Italian, after our tears, all of that gave us fits of laughter.

It took us hours to calm down: at *Harry's Bar*. We used to explore cemeteries a lot, it reassured us; we called it survivors' visits.'

Gainsbourg joked: 'I was born under a good star. Yellow.' Out of his artistic failure, after seventeen years of studying the visual arts without finding his style, and a Jewish identity that he never fully accepted, he created an art of the comeback, of distance and playfulness, of a still-unequal political irony. The union of Birkins and Gainsbourgs changes his vocabulary. The encounter with 'Djenne' reaffirms the beauty of 'Franglais' and of Anglicisms. Of *bang* and of *exit*, of *cool* and of *bathing beauty*. 'Cursed, popular, lonely, applauded, a model at times, often rejected, Serge Gainsbourg talked in interjections, borborygmi, neologisms, sarcasm, formulae, affirmations, or various imprecations and aphorisms. And each stylistic device has contributed to the hiding of its author,' the psychoanalyst Michel David writes in *Serge Gainsbourg. La scène du fantasme* (Serge Gainsbourg. The scene of fantasy).

Jane Birkin, for her part, fights for democracy, for the freedom of minorities and against imprisonment. She goes to Sarajevo, defends the Burmese Aung San Suu Kyi, the Dalai-Lama and the Tibetans. She becomes an indispensable part of cultural life, works for the survival of the Théâtre du Soleil, speaks up for its founder Ariane Mnouchkine when she needs it. In 1999, at the Avignon Festival, she creates *Arabesque*. In it, she revisits Serge Gainsbourg's repertory using Middle-Eastern sounds, a way for her to fight prejudice. 'Belonging to a mixed family has taught me a lot. It has helped me to know Serge. I didn't know any other Jews. I can see that the fact that my grandson is half-black helps me. One becomes more vigilant – otherwise I would have been any old Englishwoman. Stupid remarks like "he's a bit of a type, isn't he?" become unbearable. One is on the lookout. The French have this advantage, of being mixed.'

When the Taubira affair breaks out – François Hollande's Minister of Justice, born in Guyana, is subjected to racist slurs from militants opposed to same-sex marriage – Jane comes to her defence. 'I completely agree with her opinions as Minister of Justice. She is against routine incarceration, preferring modern means, such as the electronic bracelet. My father was a probation officer, he had volunteered for this role after the war, he, a resistance hero. He had ten children he was responsible for, and he never failed. I have demonstrated against the death penalty in Great Britain with him. I have seen unbelievable situations. One of the convicts was a pyromaniac. His mother was an undertaker. The boy saw wheelbarrows full of dead bodies arrive; she put them on the kitchen table in order to prepare them. My father thought that putting him in prison would have been nonsensical, that he was fragile and wouldn't have survived it. The mother, to thank my father, said to him: "Hey, Mister Birkin, when the terrible day comes, I'll do a great job for you!" We have to accept all of this, it is part of life.'

The family obviously has its flaws. It has a difficult heritage. Under the media spotlights, Serge and Jane had to come up with new ideas, and endure. He is a peculiar father. In 2015, Charlotte Gainsbourg left it all behind for New York with her husband and her three children. She was brought up without any restrictions concerning the time of day: free to hang out in nightclubs until dusk when her friends had to be home at midnight – one day, when she was fourteen, daddy called the nightclub *Les Bains Douches* to prevent her from entering, because he had heard that she had smoked a joint. She denied it.

At thirteen, she films the sulphurous music video 'Lemon Incest' with her father in New York. She is pathologically shy: at nine, when her parents separate, and at fourteen, when she receives the César for most promising actress for *An Impudent Girl* by Claude Miller. Before she goes on stage, her father gives her a long kiss on the mouth. Serge makes this the object of his attention in the film *Charlotte for Ever*. It is 1986, the provocateur has devoured Lucien from within.

Born in 1982 out of the union of Jane Birkin and the director Jacques Doillon, Lou has a critical view of her family, while remaining naturally kind. 'My father isn't a nice man, no more than Serge was. I come from a family of troublemakers, where women had to be muses, without the right to speak. I have never resigned myself to that,' she confides in the Spanish daily *El Pais* in 2015, on the occasion of the launch of her second album, *Lay Low*.

But what is this baroque family, where the order of generations seems to be confused? Lou Doillon has defined it thus, to *Psychologies Magazine*, in January 2013: 'It's important to understand that I come from a family that lives in the cult of Peter Pan. We all live the lives of children. Until the death of Anno [son of Andrew Birkin], when we went to Wales, we played hide and seek together, parents and children, for hours on end!'

Another example given by Lou Doillon: the plush monkey –
Munkey – who appears on the cover of the album *Histoire de
Melody Nelson*. 'My mother slept with it until Serge's death,
and she put it in his grave with him. My uncle freaked out: he
didn't want Munkey to leave! Everything is like this with us.
My mother keeps everything, our first shoes, our first teeth,
there are pictures of all of us as children all over the place … We
live in our childhood, amongst ghosts. Except my father, he's
on the other end of the spectrum, he lives in the present, open
to the world … For him, if there had to be a picture, it would
be of a tree, or of a road he finds beautiful. With my mother, on
the other hand, it's like a cult of death!'

With Jacques Doillon, Lou says, Jane is far removed from
the things she had known with Serge in the 1970s: 'this glamorous, successful life, with great financial windfalls.' Lou Doillon
feels like an intruder 'a little mongrel who wasn't part of the
royal Gainsbourg/Birkin circle, who had no understanding
whatsoever of what Charlotte had gone through. I didn't have
the same mother as Kate or Charlotte. My mother didn't appear
in the press. Serge was obsessed with success, with the media.'

Jane, in her union with Serge, with her youth, her freshness, shows the world that it is possible to transform someone
with love. And nothing can make her deviate from that idea.
In 1968, she is so touching when she smiles at him while eating
an apple in a market that he can't help embracing her! In 1990,
having been separated from him for ten years, she still smiles at
him. Serge will die a few months later, they are interviewed by
Michel Denisot for *Mon zénith à moi* on the television channel

Canal+. She brings her poetry to the television screen, stroking the hair of her ageing man, a bloated, blabbering alcoholic. She is now at the prime of her beauty, a mature woman who is preparing to return to the stage, for *Park Your Car in Harvard Yard* by Israël Horovitz. She leans against Serge's shoulder, says: 'We have Charlotte,' with that delicious hint of Franglais and that loving, soft glance. She forgives, and never judges. Devastated a moment earlier, Gainsbourg is the picture of broken humanity we all have in us. The family is never going to be divided on Jane's account.

Brigitte Bardot and Jane Birkin on the set of *Don Juan 73*, directed by Roger Vadim.

ten

Don Juan

*P*aris, Christmas 1972. *Lui*, the magazine for the modern man, publishes a series of shocking photos: Jane Birkin and Brigitte Bardot are flirting, naked, embracing. It's daring. Of course, the young Englishwoman has already offended the Vatican four years earlier, when she lasciviously sang 'Je t'aime ... moi non plus': a tale of sodomy with her lover, Serge Gainsbourg. Of course, Brigitte Bardot, a liberated woman, has already upset decorum with the films *Contempt* and *... And God Created Woman*. But ... who had this crazy idea of bedding them down in the same cabin? Who brings us two equally alluring sex symbols on a plate? A notorious macho with a Russian father, a broody, handsome man and charmer of stars: Roger Vadim.

The portfolio published in *Lui* is signed by Léonard de Raemy, a Swiss photographer and friend of Brigitte Bardot. It precedes the launch of Vadim's fifteenth feature film, *Don Juan 73*. The film deals with a case of fluctuating identity: it is also known as *If Don Juan Were a Woman ...* Or both at the same time, to be precise.

Bardot is Jeanne, a feminine Don Juan, who seduces and destroys. In the relevant scene, she rolls around in the marital sheets of an idiot she wants to humiliate by seducing his very young wife, Clara. Hence, Jane.

Don Juan 73 is based on a script of sketches, dotted with symbols of fashion and modernity. Brigitte Bardot, the icon of femininity, begins her adventure of lesbian seduction during a very fashionable drinks party: outfitted in an evening dress and an orange cape by Givenchy, she is on the arm of Clara/Jane, who is very scantily clad by Loris Azzaro, the inventor of Tina Turner's lurex knit and chain dresses, as well as the famous dress that opens down the front into three rings, pioneered by the top model Marisa Berenson. Faced with the vulgarity of a domineering husband, Clara, the ingénue, engages in a conversation with the older, experienced woman:

> CLARA: I think all men are a bit savage, don't you?
> JEANNE: No – I, for one, have been somewhat
>   civilized.
> CLARA: But you're not …
> JEANNE: A man? Oh yes, in a different life.
> CLARA: Was that a long time ago?
> JEANNE: Not really. About 400 years, or thereabouts.
>   That was a great time to be alive in Spain. I was a
>   rich and courageous aristocrat, and I seduced all the
>   women … I was young. I died at 30.

Jeanne/Brigitte inverses the gender and the genres. Clara/Jane doesn't seem too concerned. What's her reply? 'I suppose it's true that people died young at the time …'

Ah! The innocence of girls! Ah! The magic of the cinema, playground of changing appearances and twisted loves!

For Bardot, trailblazer of the liberation of the body, the film didn't present much of a problem. 'In Brigitte's mind, sex isn't synonymous with sin, she's a stranger to the Judeo-Christian psychological hodgepodge that comes with the idea of pleasure,' her ex-husband Roger Vadim writes in one of his numerous autobiographical books, *From One Star to the Next*. Nevertheless, *Don Juan 73* ends up outing her from the cinema altogether. On the other hand, Jane had already been seen naked – or near-naked – by 1972. On film, and on dozens of magazine covers, be they newspapers, or men's or women's magazines, which she has graced with her gauche and sparkling allure, with her youth and her smile, since her encounter with Serge Gainsbourg. She has revealed herself on glossy paper, from her blue-green eyes to her sloping, long neck, from her flat but sensual torso to her graceful ankles.

Today she thinks that *Don Juan 73* is rubbish, and she can laugh about it. And yet, Bardot and Birkin in bed, that's no small thing! Vadim has chosen to imagine a sapphic scene. That's not really surprising for a seducer of his stripe. These two flirting beauties are a pretty seductive sight. The idea of the character of Don Juan dates back to 1630, thanks to the pen of the Spanish playwright Tirso de Molina. 'Don Juan is a violator of the morals of his time,' the director explains. A favourite target of American feminists since his marriage to Jane Fonda, he wants a feminine Don Juan. What's more, even if one includes Rainer Werner Fassbinder's *The Bitter Tears of Petra von Kant*, one could count the mainstream films featuring lesbian scenes so far on the fingers of one hand.

This crazy idea grants us the sight of these two little slips of a thing, one atop the other. Everything seems weightless. Bardot leans on Jane's elongated back. One is a graceful girl, the other lays bare her voluptuous curves. Brigitte Bardot kisses her. Cornered, Jane escapes, a light blue gaze, a full mouth, she's like a little rabbit caught in the headlights. 'Be erotic, be erotic,' Birkin repeats ironically, as if a male voice whispered reproaches to her. The script isn't without its weaknesses.

In the background, the intertwined figures are multiplied by mirrors. Thanks to an optical effect that's caused by a wall mirror, an impression of horizontally-stacked naked bodies is created, an ochre pile, and it isn't quite clear whether it's an orgy or a mass grave. Our two heroines frolic among all this strangeness.

In any case, everything seems uncanny. Since the intention of the scene is bizarre, it would even be perverse, if not for the libertarian era of its creation. The characters reunited here are the heroes of a real-life turbulent love story: Jane Birkin lives with Serge Gainsbourg, who is the former lover of Brigitte Bardot, who, in turn, used to be the wife and muse of Vadim.

Seen from that angle, the sapphic scene in the female *Don Juan* verges on a foursome in the sense described by Yvette Gilbert, the 'fin de siècle truthsayer', *grande dame* of modern French *chanson* – the art practiced by the handsome Serge. A friend of Sigmund Freud, she made fun, in 1885, of the Boudins and the Boutons, innocent swingers:

It was Monsieur Bouton's profession to sell strings of
sausages / Monsieur Boudin, on the other hand, sold
strings of buttons.

Professionally, Serge, Roger, Brigitte and Jane are artists. They
present themselves as being far removed from the soup of
middle-class life. After four years of living together, what has
happened to the loves of Jane and Serge? Serge Gainsbourg,
provocateur, lover of aphorisms, had one day written in the
margins of a notebook: 'I will no longer make love, apart from
by force,' before getting lost in his romance with Brigitte Bardot
and falling for an Englishwoman in a miniskirt, twenty years
his junior. What a mix-up!

We would like to distract ourselves from this, and turn a
page. To carry on with attempting to chronicle the loves of Jane
and Serge. But the scene is captivating, it keeps us spellbound.
Beneath the eyes of Roger and Serge, two shadowy men, Jane:
snuggling in Bardot's arms – a sizzling sensual fantasy – hums a
Scottish lullaby. An image whose verso, with which it is closely
related, reveals an extreme amorous density. At the beginning
of the 1970s, the staging of one's own life is an essential part of
celebrity – this absolute dictatorship that has been exposed by
Andy Warhol.

Is Gainsbourg through with Bardot? The response
turns out to be difficult, and the question hard to formulate.
First of all, there are many phantoms: Maurice Ronet, actor;
Michel Magne, composer; Roger Vadim, director; Jean Cau,
scriptwriter; Léonard de Raemy, photographer; Suzanne

Durrenberger, script supervisor, who left all her notebooks to the Cinémathèque Française – apart from the one that dealt with *Don Juan 73*. Probably because *Don Juan 73* was of little consequence compared to the great films Suzanne Durrenberger has worked on, from Vadim's first features to the masterpieces of Buñuel and all the way up to the films of Patrice Chéreau.

And then there are the voids that result from the passage of time. The film's lead actor, Robert Hossein, born in 1927, is tired. Brigitte Bardot, a recluse in Saint-Tropez, tells us she can't remember anything about it at all. One thing is certain: she didn't come across Serge Gainsbourg on the set. And yet, we must try to understand the interwoven cinematographic and passionate circumstances that link Bardot and Birkin. We ask Jane: what might all this mean? What do these mixed-up passions, these broken couples, these compelling love stories, these role-playing games, the constant staging of a reality lived on the edge tell us?

Forty-four years later, Jane Birkin has a simple view of the story. Putting the novice and the icon into bed together is just a great marketing idea. Vadim excels at this. The smart Vadim wanted to bring the 'star and the little newcomer' together, she says bluntly. 'At a later date, he would have hired Kate Moss and me.'

On the set of *Don Juan*, Jane Birkin discovers that she shares a certain social unselfconsciousness with Bardot: 'Her lack of ambition was disarming, which I found wonderful. I didn't have any ambition either … It was my luck to meet people who had it in my place.' Birkin isn't as naïve as she sometimes pretends. We insist: wasn't Vadim thinking about the amorous links that underpinned the relationships between him, his actors and their lovers? 'Deep down, I don't know,' Jane answers, her glance hovering over her glasses. We ask another great lady who has played a role in the life of Serge Gainsbourg. Aged 86, the rarely-heard voice of Juliette Gréco cuts, in an old-fashioned way: 'Vadim is a pimp.'

On the occasion of *Don Juan*, Jane uncovers the body of the woman who was and remained her rival: it is perfect. Not a wrinkle, not a blemish. She looks for one, but in vain. Brigitte Bardot has such beautiful feet that Jane asks Vadim and the cameraman to film them intertwined with her own, to create the impression that these feet belong to the less-than-perfect Jane. Birkin has experienced a London full of free love, where Anita Pallenberg, Marianne Faithfull, Keith Richards and Mick Jagger interweave their beds and artificial highs without much hesitation. Bardot is 38, she is escaping from a stifling generation. Vadim gives us a new fictional equation: Bardot + Birkin = BB.

On the set of *Don Juan 73*, someone – but who? – asks Jane to sing a post-coital song. It's a spontaneous idea, not in the initial script. Jane thinks it was Bardot herself who suggested it in order to ease the atmosphere. 'She was sweet, she said to me: "How do you think we should do it? Do you want to sing a song?"' Playful, perhaps with a hint of perversity, Bardot suggests 'Je t'aime … moi non plus'. Jane Birkin still shudders at the thought of this highly delicate situation. One can easily imagine that Birkin is petrified at the idea of singing the line '*I go, I go and I come, inside of you,*' that was dedicated to BB. '*Help!*', Birkin sighs, rolling her eyes, with the distance created by her age.

And all of a sudden, on the set of *Don Juan*, Birkin says that 'her blood runs cold.' In order to preserve the harmony between her body and that of her rival, she sings. She has a troubled look, but she is clever. She saves herself, as she will sing with Mickey 3D, in 2003, in the very truthful song 'Je m'appelle Jane' (My Name is Jane):

> Tell me, Birkin, why do you never get upset / Is it that you run away from anger?' / It's just that I am fragile.

Introverted, she comes up with an alternative proposition, opting for 'the most familial of all the genres, the ditty': why not 'My Bonnie Lies Over the Ocean'? 'which my mother sang to me when I was little. The mistress of Bonnie Prince Charlie waits for his return, but he won't come back.' She finally goes for 'Oh My Darling Clementine', an American folk ballad. Hummed, the sad story of the gold digger whose daughter has fallen into a mineshaft is not without its share of humour.

This scene of feigned love is perfect. Multifaceted. Celebrity prevents the truth of hard facts and Jane Birkin never wanted to chip away at the image of Serge. So we remained in the dark until now. Today Birkin tells all, there is no longer any risk in doing so. Gainsbourg is an icon, so is she. If she had such a fresh and youthful face, it was because she had cried all night. 'They couldn't do my make-up, I was all shiny. When one cries a lot, the morning after is a disaster. I had bulbous, shiny eyes. This gave me a look that was so astonishingly fresh because suddenly it prevented them from using all that sixties stuff they would otherwise have wanted to put on me. With a fringe and all that, the effect would have been quite different.' But thanks to her tears, a 'very youthful look is created, and Brigitte was sublime.'

'Poor' Bardot, systematically subjected to wigs and 'very ugly' make-up, contrasts with 'the person she is as she arrives on the set: so pretty.' Bardot, in turn, has also been crying until dawn because Vadim, Jane explains, 'has made her life hell all night.' He said horrible things about her, her career, her acting and her life. And Jane, why has she cried? 'Because Serge had beaten me up. I ran away, escaping to the hotel.' Really beaten her up? 'Yes.' Why? 'Because he was jealous. Terribly jealous.' Of Brigitte Bardot? 'Not at all, Serge was mad with jealousy, suspicious of Vadim. Vadim was very flirtatious, and I may have been, too. I wasn't an angel, but I didn't deserve that, that much is for sure.'

In the script, Jeanne, who is the enemy of Louis Prévost, the vulgar husband, delivers the final blow in London, where she has agreed to follow the couple, but under one condition: that they take the ferry-boat. Prévost has some erotic dreams in his first-class cabin and BB/Jeanne takes the opportunity to lead Jane/Clara out on deck, whispering sweet nothings into her ear. The two friends sneak out, they pinch some drinks from the bar. And they kiss. Bardot in her pyjamas, at sunrise, embracing Birkin among the seagulls and lifeboats, it's a tender scene. Once they arrive in London, they obviously end up in bed together.

The ferry-boat, however, is really Serge's territory. In 1969, he has dedicated 'Soixante-neuf, année érotique' to his young muse:

> Gainsbourg and his Gainsborough / Have taken the
> ferry-boat / From their bed, through the porthole /
> They look at the coast / They love each other, and the
> journey / Will take a whole year / They triumph over
> evil spells / Until nineteen-seventy.

The idea of Vadim setting foot on board makes him choleric.

To make matters worse, the shooting of *Don Juan 73* comes after the difficult summer they had spent in 1972. The couple have rented the Château Volterra, at Cap Camarat in the Gulf of Saint-Tropez, in order to gather together the Ginsburgs and the Birkins: fathers, mothers, brothers, sisters, children, nephews, nieces … Idyllic? No, Marie-Dominique Lelièvre writes in *Gainsbourg Unfiltered*: 'The Anglo-Saxon clan faces the Slav branch, led by the uncompromising Olga Ginsburg. Serge's mother does her best to make these holidays difficult, keeping a sharp eye on household stocks, as if rationing was about to make a comeback at any moment.' Jane, Serge and his dog Nana leave to join Vadim and his gang.

Serge Gainsbourg still hasn't got over the commercial failure of his album *Histoire de Melody Nelson* (The Tale of Melody Nelson), which was released in 1971. He assembles his holy trifecta: sex, cigarettes and alcohol, all in large amounts. 'He was in a very bad mood. I'm not even sure I told him there was going to be a nude scene with BB. It's the ferry-boat that caused all the trouble, because there were very few cabins and he thought Vadim could have his way with me given the circumstances.' However, on the day of shooting the lesbian scene, Serge isn't there. 'This had nothing to do with Bardot,' Jane repeats. 'He must have thought that BB and me together was a good idea.' He must have thought he'd finally overcome the crisis.

Was putting Jane and Brigitte into the same bed an exorcism? For Jane Birkin, that summed it up: she discovers that Bardot inspires jealousy, 'while my feelings more closely resembled sympathy.' She realises that Bardot is hypersensitive. On the set of *Don Juan*, nothing is easy. Vadim is being odious. At times, 'Brigitte didn't even make the first cut. She was crying. I had Kate, and there was Vadim's child, Vanessa [daughter of Jane Fonda]. Bardot had left the set and went towards her van, and I could hear some women in the street, who said: "Look how she's aged, look how ugly she is!" And I realised how much animosity people had against her. I had never known such animosity, because I was with Serge, I was so visibly with someone, that I was covered. She represented a danger to couples – I didn't.'

For a long time, Brigitte Bardot hasn't been entirely her own woman. At an early stage, she experienced the bitter taste of popular judgement. In 1961, for example, while disappointing the millions of French people who fantasised over her relationship with the handsome Jacques Charrier, she left on the arm of Samy Frey. The countless insults, by letter and in the street, ended up making her slit her wrists after a jarful of pills.

At the end of 1967, Gunter Sachs, who has been Bardot's husband for a few months, knows everything about popular hatred. When BB records the single 'Je t'aime … moi non plus' with Serge Gainsbourg, the German playboy threatens to create an international scandal. He knows exactly what he is talking about. Bardot is a sex-bomb, and if he had wanted to, he could have been the fuse to turn the actress' life into a pile of ruins.

Jane and Serge photographed by Bert Stern for *Vogue* in 1970.
(Photo by Bert Stern/Condé Nast via Getty Images)

eleven

Don Juan, Vadim and the defeat of the male

•••

*B*rigitte Bardot might have come across Jane Birkin at the 1967 Cannes Film Festival, when Antonioni's *Blow-Up* won the Palme d'Or. In this film, the public is treated to a scandalous scene that will soon attain mythical status. Jane Birkin, Gillian Hills – the London 'it girl' for the French magazine *Salut les copains* – and David Hemmings engage in a trio of sexual games. At the beginning of the sequence, the fashion photographer Thomas (Hemmings) pulls off his young model's dress. Then the two girls invert the roles: they roll their partner on the ground, undressing him in the process.

Today, this would be considered an act of sexual aggression. But in the early sixties, a girl who does not go along with male advances is considered a cow. Paradoxically, the sequence, a very far cry indeed from the pornography tolerated today, is now preceded by a parental advisory notice on YouTube. But there are no genitals on display, the only scandal being some pubic hair that can be seen in the film.

For Vadim, the object of the provocation is nudity, more than homoeroticism or sex.

He had experimented with it in his film ... *And God Created Woman*, where Bardot appears naked.

The bare backsides of Birkin and Bardot offend the magazine *Playboy*, which refuses to publish the pictures that had appeared in *Lui*. Jane Birkin smiles at a memory: in 1965, her husband John Barry had angrily dared her to strip for Antonioni – she, who always switched off their bedroom lights! He had said: 'You'll never manage it.' But she'd really gone for it.

Nudity is a major art form. Gainsbourg, a painter, knows this. He drew from life at the Paris Academy, the Beaux-Arts, was obsessed with Titian's *Pardo Venus*, and Lucas Cranach the Elder's *Eve*. In the latter painting, Eve holds the apple in her right hand and an olive twig in her left, lightly covering her nudity. In bed, where the scene of seduction unfolds, BB/Don Juan smokes and holds her cigarette, her hand conveniently placed before Jane's pudenda. On the tanned body of the svelte Englishwoman, the outline of a swimming costume is visible. This comes across as bad taste in 21st-century France, which otherwise totally lacks in modesty. At the time, a woman would take off the top of her bikini and only keep on her bottoms.

For Brigitte Bardot, *Don Juan 73* marks her swansong. She wants to leave the film business behind, tired of playing her own role *ad nauseam*. Apart from the dull *Edifying and Joyous Story of Colinot* by Nina Companeez, which was filmed in the same year, *Don Juan 73* is her final film.

'It's understandable that she's bored in this [very] soft porn that's typical of the early seventies, and whose main achievement is to have preceded such blockbusters as *Bilitis* and *Emmanuelle*,' writes Yves Bigot. 'Slightly slurring as a result of the anti-depressants she takes, and the litres of champagne and red wine she puts away, dumped by the barman Christian Kalt …' (her new passion).

In *Don Juan 73*, Vadim and the dialogue writer – the author Jean Cau – endeavour to describe a social breakdown: that of the male. Louis Prévost is the caricature of a stupid man, master of his wife Clara, and owner of the lighter she uses to light his cigar like a slave.

Don Juan 73 also marks the beginning of the end of the jet set's golden age, which it portrays in an unflattering light. The Bardot-Birkin-Hossein scene begins at les Halles, the old market of Paris, which was then under demolition. Here's the scene Vadim wrote:

```
Somewhere near the Saint Eustace Church, in
the meat section of the market, where there
are still one or two restaurants that stay
open until morning. A mixed crowd. At the bar:
workmen in long, blood-stained white work
```

coats, some local regulars, a few drunks who
are more-or-less tolerated …

Inside the restaurant: meat salesmen, and
from time to time typical Parisians, restoring
themselves with an onion soup or a pepper steak
after a heavy night …

At one of the tables, there's a merry and
agitated group: the star dancers of an English
ballet ensemble, celebrating their opening
night with some friends. Among them, fresh and
full of laughter despite the time of night [the
sun is coming up] we encounter JEANNE.

The plot strands then come together at the apartment of Louis
Prévost (Hossein) and his wife Clara (Birkin), whose Rolls
Jeanne has spotted between two meat counters.

The terrace is located at the top of a large
building [maybe at Saint-Cloud], overlooking the
whole of Paris. At the centre of the terrace
there's a pool, where a heart adorned with
flowers and large artificial water lilies float.
There are flowers everywhere, excessively so.
Prévost gives a party for his wife's birthday.

All the guests [some 40 of them] are in
evening dress and black tie, except for some
young people whose appearance is less formal,
but very fashionable.

Prévost, for his part, sports a kind of
elegant high-collared Russian jacket made of
black silk.

Buffet and drinks, butlers, musicians,
pillows covered in Indian silk, fur coats, etc.
The whole setting could be in bad taste, but
its extravagance hides the 'new money' aspect
in an almost baroque atmosphere.

'What does the husband do?' Jeanne wants to know. Clara has 'one day' asked him the same question. '"But what is it you sell, what do you buy, darling? …" And he answered: "Me? How would I know, I never see the merchandise! A great business-man does business, that's all!"'

The husband lives in London. That's where the defeat of the male takes shape. Jeanne sleeps with his wife, but he is una-ware. Sexism is at its zenith. In the lobby, he shows a picture of Bardot/Jeanne climbing the stairs of the ferry-boat (out of focus, of course: his wife took the picture) to his guests, two white male Americans. He comments: 'Not bad! Huh? Very good fam-ily! Good pedigree! … A magnificent stride! A total winner in bed!' (and, in English, with a bad accent): '*Good fuck: I bet you!*'

The phone rings in the bedroom, but goes unanswered. 'Madame doesn't answer the phone,' mutters the butler. No, Madame is kissing, she is cuddled against the shoulder of the woman he takes for a thoroughbred filly. Madame takes revenge and indulges herself. Prévost/Hossein enters the scene, in charge; he is looking forward to a hot threesome. Fops look at and compliment themselves in the mirror. The Louis Prévost of *Don Juan 73* contemplates himself as he undresses. He perfumes himself, studies his profile, his forehead and torso, he thinks he is about to join two sublime creatures in bed and give them a good seeing to.

Louis sings a tango at the top of his voice, 'Adieu Paris', the satirical French version of a tango by Carlos Gardel: 'Adios muchachos', performed in 1937 by Berthe Silva. That's not in the original script. Someone had the idea of adding it in spontaneously, because love and song are two sides of the same coin. Robert Hossein has a full voice. He is handsome, he intones:

> Good bye Paris, I am retiring to the countryside / I've
> had enough of dining the chicks / And walking home
> on a pavement that's like the rough seas.

And, at the same time, Birkin slips on a pair of jeans, Bardot a dress. They leave him. The man is flabbergasted. He beats Bardot, she bleeds. Jane hasn't done up her top, she has a touchingly boyish chest. She has an astonished gaze, she appears dazed and subdued, but shows a little vengeful smile.

Where are they on the scale of alienation? In the 1970s, Jane does not fear scandal. For example, in 1974, she poses naked for *Lui*. Gainsbourg sorts out all the details. He writes a little poem, 'Une Jane nue':

Antibardot, antifonda / A bit Antinous, Antinea / Jane,
my little androgyne / They'll love you / Neither will
they, pin you up / Next to Mick Jagger and Marilyn.

He guides her, she is tied to a bed, he pulls her by her hair, she is
in a nightie and boots, and her legs are spread apart. The pictures
are signed Francis Giacobetti, the photographer 'of the sexual
revolution'. Jane and Serge play the game of celebrity. They know
all about appearances. But this is just noise. The gist is elsewhere.

When he films *Don Juan*, Roger Vadim has just left another
Jane and fallen in love with Catherine, heiress of the Schneider
steel-making empire. He is a ladies' man. After BB, he has married Jane Fonda, 27 at the time, in 1967. Five years of living
with the French director turned the actress into a feminist. Her
description, in her autobiography *My Life So Far*, published in
2005, of Vadim as a sex addict, exposes her ex-husband like a
butterfly on a wheel. First of all, she writes, he explains to her
that jealousy is a bourgeois concept. That having sex with others
isn't a betrayal. And the starlets are on parade. He repeats to
all and sundry that 'the chains of marriage are so heavy that it
takes three to carry them.' Then he spices up their lovemaking
by singing the praises of Madame Claude's prostitutes, or of
girls he meets for casual encounters. 'That really hurt me …
it reinforced my notion that I wasn't good enough. I thought
that if I said no, he'd leave me, and I couldn't imagine myself
without him.' She ended up leaving.

Vadim failed to hold on to Jane Fonda, so he created
Barbarella for her in 1968. The heroine is struggling against a

devilish orgasmic machine that is meant to kill her with excessive pleasure. But Barbarella's capacity for pleasure overwhelms the mechanics of the deadly contraption, and ends up frying its circuits. Jane Fonda is very erotic in this science-fiction role. The film bestows on Vadim the loathing of American feminist movements, the admiration of pop culture enthusiasts, and the attention of Linda Williams, an American theoretician, who originated *porn studies*. According to the researcher, this film represents the first attempt to show the female multiple orgasm on screen, confirming the notion that 'the more a woman makes love, the more she can, and the more can, the more she wants.'

If *Don Juan 73* is formally far from perfect, its dialogues are interesting. It is a new collaboration between Jean Cau and Vadim, who last worked together on *The Game Is Over*, an adaption of a novel by Zola, that featured Jane Fonda in the lead role. Jean-Paul Sartre's erstwhile personal assistant is a pure product of post-war Saint-Germain-des-Prés, where Raymond Queneau, Juliette Gréco, Jean-Paul Sartre, Simone de Beauvoir, Boris Vian and a whole left-wing 'tribe' of poets and intellectuals striving to liberate the era's morals congregated. But, in 1973, the Gaullist Jean Cau has turned. He's gone over to the right. He has published *Stables of the Occident, A Moral Treatise*. The literary critic of *L'Express*, Angelo Rinaldi, comments: 'This is not the first time that, *en route*, the left has lost the talented son of a worker, whom society has accepted at the banquet by way of exception, and who leaves the table, roaming aimlessly and burping with satiation.'

Unfazed, Jean Cau, friend of Alain Delon, bemoans the 'decadence' of contemporary civilisation.

Wherein lies morality and decadence in 1973? First of all, it is the time-honoured attack on religious morality. When Jane Birkin ends up in Brigitte Bardot's bed, this happens as a result of a turbulent decade, characterised by the cult of celebrity, when the anti-clerical movement played a significant role. *Don Juan 73* does not incur the wrath of the Vatican, which was so appalled by the sighs and allusions to sodomy contained in 'Je t'aime … moi non plus' four years earlier. And yet, the film starts with an iconoclastic scene: the funeral of one Berthe, in a cathedral, to the strains of Mozart's 'Requiem'. The priest reads from St John's Gospel. Obligatory passage: 'Let whoever is without sin cast the first stone.'

Strange close-ups: in the church pews there are, the script indicates:

```
whores, nothing but whores, some two hundred
of them, who have come here to lay their
"patriarch", Berthe, to rest …
```

Strange faces, an idiot with false teeth, a black woman wearing too much make-up.

```
Wilted faces, young ones and old ones.
Crumbling make-up from the previous night.
Some have come without taking the time to put
make-up on, with the blinking eyes of nocturnal
birds one points a torch at.
```

The handsome priest is Jeanne's cousin and she is in love with him. She wants to confess, herself, but he has 'other things to do than to listen to the tale of [her] baseness.' He does listen to her, though, and ends up yielding to temptation.

The defeat of the male is not Serge Gainsbourg's concern. He is different! Birkin and Bardot have understood this. He also knows it. At Rue de Verneuil, he has pinned the famous picture of his two lovers in bed to the wall. It was precious to him. As a voyeur? Maybe. As an artist? Certainly. *Don Juan 73* was an exception, where Gainsbourg was conspicuously absent. For he was always present at Jane's sets: 'He worked at my shoots, in hotel rooms, or on his knees. So my trailers have served a purpose! They allowed him to write. Serge insisted on joining me, because, thinking my films were 'aphrodisiac', he feared I might go off with an actor who was better looking than him. Once he was there, he was bored stiff. I remember a film we shot in Oxford [*May Morning*, a swinging hippie film by Ugo Liberatore, released in 1970]. I had booked a very nice hotel I knew thanks to my father, the *Albert*. Serge was writing

"Melody" all day long. A few years later, I worked on another shoot, in Milan [*Burnt by a Scalding Passion*, by Giorgio Capitani, an almost farcical film], Serge was furious when he discovered the out-of-town hotel I had taken. The bath tub – communal and missing a plug – was at the end of a long corridor. A construction site under our windows made a terrible racket. Serge rented the room opposite, which contained a fire extinguisher.

'The album *L'homme À Tête De Chou* [The Man With The Cabbage Head] – which contains the song "Fire Extinguisher Murder" – is written here. In the daytime, Serge wrote. In the evening, he joined us and clowned around. With saucepans ferreted out from the kitchens, he turned himself into a one-man band. My brother Andrew accompanied him. We all howled with laughter. On these sets, we all dressed up. The boys made themselves up like girls. And, at the same time, Serge could, from one moment to the next, break into tears, as he had done in Paris, for 24 hours, in front of a candle, because he thought I'd gone back to England for good after the filming of *Slogan*.'

After the red warning signs of Saint-Tropez, *Don Juan* really does sound the alarm bells. The passionate and jealous upheaval of *Don Juan 73* affords Serge Gainsbourg the time to write Jane's first album, *Di doo dah*. But probably also a first draft of 'Je suis venu te dire que je m'en vais' (I've Come To Tell You That I'm Going Away), the prelude to a future breakup. This is also a song with a yet more sinister premonition: in May 1973, Serge suffers a heart attack that almost kills him. Rushed to the American Hospital in Paris, he calls a press conference to be photographed surrounded by his favourite poison, *Gitane* cigarettes, while Jane fights for an elusive sobriety.

Don Juan 73 represents a key moment in the story of Jane and Serge, an obscure limit that Jane analyses in *Boxes*, the feature film she directs in 2007 – its narrative showcasing her two parents, her three daughters and her three husbands: the cruel John Barry, the genius Serge Gainsbourg, and the unfaithful Jacques Doillon. When is the spell finally broken? The director of photography on *Boxes*, who is also Jane's friend, sums it up thus: 'How long does a beginning last?'

Jane poses with the plush toy, Munkey for the cover of
Gainsbourg's seminal album: L'Histoire de Melody Nelson, in 1971.
(Photo by Giancarlo BOTTI/Gamma-Rapho via Getty Images)

twelve

Androgyny: the foundations of the Republic

∙∙∙

*G*ainsbourg is a bruised man. To begin with, Jane dresses his wounds, and her own. 'This was done with tenderness. In the space of a year, he was over his hurt. And so was I. He thought of himself as ugly, I found him handsome.' What did Jane bring into Serge's life? We ask Régine. 'Freshness, a lightness of being. When she arrived in Paris, without speaking a word of French, she was candid, refined, *eccentric* and amusing. She was also strong and intelligent. She was totally unpretentious and one of the most beautiful women in the world.'

Jane loved the b-sides of Serge's records. She had the hidden side. 'He was mine, as a secret, before he went platinum with *Aux armes et cætera*, in 1979. When I was young, I had a parrot, Polly; it was horrible to everyone. With me it was docile. And I had the good luck of having Ginsburg, who had the beauty of Kafka.'

'Serge,' Jane continues, 'made me sing one octave higher than my normal voice, which made me sound like a choirboy at church.' Yes, but what does she mean by that? And, conversely, what did she give to him? She isn't clear about this, and that's fine, since she is alert to all the signs that usher in the great revolutions. Once again: what has she given him? Masterpieces.

The first: the new version of 'Je t'aime … moi non plus'. When he offers her the song, Jane accepts immediately. It's one more gift. She accepts out of jealousy, she says, so that he wouldn't offer it to anyone else. After Bardot left him, Serge did the rounds of London clubs, chatting up young blondes, with the recording of a 'bombshell' of a song thrown in. This anecdote amuses Marianne Faithful, figurehead of Swinging London, who appeared in the musical *Anna*. Faithfull isn't Gainsbourg's type: a generous chest, she's a rocker by character, a serious addict with a raw, deep voice. Mick Jagger's friend doesn't fall for this fragile *Frenchie*, either. But she loved the artist Gainsbourg, whose 'Lola Rastaquouère' she covered, and whom she asked, in 1982, to direct two videos for her album *Dangerous Acquaintances*.

So, Jane Birkin gets hold of 'Je t'aime … moi non plus', and the song conquers the world: precisely because it combines innocence and perversity. Serge Gainsbourg gets hold of Birkin's voice. In that environment, Jane is a revolution. 'I gave my very high-pitched voice to Serge, anyway,' Birkin concedes. Anyway. 'Then he started using a kind of recitative. That's because of me, I always hesitate to say so, and it's also because of his age: he now thought of himself as a Russian poet with his small glasses, I loved that.' Borrowed from the great tradition of French *chanson réaliste*, Serge Gainsbourg's spoken-word singing is reminiscent of the repetitive, rhythmical recitative style of Jewish *cantors*.

For Gainsbourg, 'Je t'aime … moi non plus' is both a burden and an opportunity not to pass up. The song is recorded at London's Marble Arch Studio. Each records their sighs in separate booths and Gainsbourg mixes them as conductor. On returning to Paris, Jane and Serge test the water. They're staying at a hotel, on the Rue des Beaux-Arts, the place in which Oscar Wilde died. At its plush restaurant, Serge plays the record as a surprise. Forks freeze in mid-air. He knows he's got a hit. When Jane plays the song to her parents, before the single is released, she makes sure to lift the needle from the disc at the most explicit passages.

Less than a year after May 1968, the song explodes all over the place. The radio stations refuse to play it, with the exception of France Inter, thanks to José Artur, the host of *Pop Club*. But the outrageous slow dance is played a lot in nightclubs. 'The Pope has been our best publicist,' Jane remembers. The *Osservatore Romano*, the Vatican's official publication, succeeds in stopping the Italian distribution of the song which it considers obscene. The boss of the Italian subsidiary of Philips is taken into provisional detention. In Great Britain, the BBC boycotts the song. Despite that, the single reaches the top of the English charts, a first for a French production.

Following the furore caused by 'Je t'aime … moi non plus', Georges Meyerstein-Maigret, the boss of Philips, summons the 'couple of the year'. He tells them: 'Listen, chaps, I'm happy to go to prison, but for an LP, not a single.' Gainsbourg now creates the album, *Jane Birkin/Serge Gainsbourg*, which will be banned for minors and sold under cellophane. He brings together some published songs ('Élisa', 'Les Sucettes', 'Sous le soleil exactement'), some film compositions, including the title song for *Slogan*, and two songs for Jane: 'Soixante-neuf, année érotique' and 'Jane B'. This last song is a pastiche on a poem by Nabokov, which appears in *Lolita*. To accommodate Jane's high pitch, he borrows the melody from Frédéric Chopin's 'Prelude n° 4, Opus 28'. A first version mentioned a wicker basket, a key worn as a pendant: a lucky charm he has given her – he wears the same. It also describes a murdered woman, who is asleep 'with a handkerchief between her teeth', 'her skirt torn, ripped off, rolled up'.

And then? I insist: Jane, what did you give him? 'I gave him the three-day stubble, like make-up. His beard didn't grow thick. He had a *Brown* shaver that didn't shave much. It kept just enough stubble. This accentuated his face very well. He looked a little bit Tartar, whereas, when he took it all off, he was too smooth.'

Serge Gainsbourg has jug ears. His mother tries an experiment with Jane: sticking them to his head with adhesive tape. The result is ugly; the triangular harmony of the face is broken. Jane has seen the videos shot with Brigitte Bardot before their encounter. She finds him exquisite. There's nothing to change. 'He was perfect, which was probably the result of an age that suited him much better, 40 years.' With hindsight, she can now see stages of his transformation. His dishevelled look on the cover of *Manon*, which was released in March 1968, two months before they met. 'He wasn't smooth. There was great beauty.

The super-eight footage brings it out very well. There still was some more to do – taking off the socks, finding slippers and jewellery.'

She liked neither 'underpants for boys', nor socks, so she suggested he should wear jeans 'with nothing underneath'. One day, she goes to Repetto, in Rue de la Paix. She is in search of ballet flats. She's in the right place: the brand was created in 1947 by Rose Repetto, mother of the ballet director and chore-ographer Roland Petit. Repetto redesigns the tip and invents the famous Cendrillon ballet flats: they're red, open to the toes, ordered by Brigitte Bardot, who wears them in 1956, in Vadim's ... *And God Created Woman*.

'I saw a pair of soft shoes in a sales basket and called Serge for his size.' They're *Zizis*: slim white Oxfords that Rose Repetto has designed for Zizi Jeanmaire, her daughter-in-law. Roland Petit and Zizi Jeanmaire are a great couple. Serge Gainsbourg is their friend. For the star dancer-turned-showgirl, he com-poses songs that are performed on television, such as 'Élisa', a military march. The Birkin-Gainsbourgs spend bright summers with the Petits, who have acquired a house in the Malmousque area of Marseille, on the Corniche. Laughter, scooter outings, delirious creativity that culminates in the show *Zizi, je t'aime!* performed in 1971 at the Casino de Paris, 'with choreography by Roland Petit, costumes by Yves Saint Laurent, and a stage designed by the Russian Erté. There was a real train, and Zizi walked around in King Kong's hand, it was fabulous,' Jane says.

But, as she rummages in this unisex basket, she still doesn't know who's who in this directory of the popular arts. 'The ballet shoes the boys wore were incredibly soft – men's ballet shoes; one can't walk a lot in them, but Serge didn't walk, he took taxis. There were lots of happy coincidences. After that, seeing his slender ankles was perfectly enchanting. The socks had to go in order to reveal his slender ankles.' Gainsbourg's chest is hairless. 'I loved his nose, his mouth, his eyes, and the absence of body hair was delicious!' 'That's what I've given him,' she says. 'Femininity.'

'And then, with his long hair, he became irresistible.' To this she adds: 'the jewellery on his wrists, the diamonds, the sapphires that suited him so well and that I bought near the Rue de Rivoli: countess diamonds.' He could have had more of them, Jane remarks. But much of his jewellery got stolen, 'the little diamonds, the little things I gave him at the beginning.'

On the morning of New Year's Day 1973, Jane Birkin sees her Serge come home in tears, and her brother Andrew distressed. They have celebrated the New Year at Pigalle. Some boys, whose bad intentions he didn't perceive, embrace him to wish him a happy New Year. Serge thought 'they were his groupies, and that may even have been the case.' On the phone, Jane tells the police station that he followed them into their car and that they've stolen all his jewellery, that he's upset, because he has none left. Charming, the policeman advises her: 'Tell Monsieur Gainsbourg that he shouldn't enter a car with people he doesn't know.' It would have been funny, had Serge not been so down. Andrew, a photographer, has taken pictures of the amicable goings-on in the bar with 'the guys who were about to steal his jewellery. That's really funny.' Andrew then ran after the car, he saw the false number plate fall. Serge is furious, calls him a coward because he hasn't followed the thugs.

'And somehow this suited me well, because, all of a sudden, I could start again with a clean slate. I bought a midnight-blue sapphire, it was almost black, and there were tiny little diamonds all around it, and then, at the same time I found the bracelet of an old Russian countess, with sapphires and old diamonds, which was also beautiful. Because he wasn't hairy. On a hairy guy, it would have looked like a chain bracelet, but he had the skin of a very, very pale countess. No hair, and a personal delicacy that was absolutely refined and splendid.' When was this? Jane's memory can play tricks on her. When it comes to time, to dates, but never when it comes to the details she's seen. 'You can see it on the pictures, because afterwards, it was a sapphire. And then, this was the time he wore this English girls' jacket, just before the famous cover with the monkeys.' In other words: before the release of the album with scatological schoolboy tendencies, *Vue de l'Extérieur* (Seen From the Outside), which includes 'Je suis venu te dire que je m'en vais', a song Gainsbourg started working on while Jane Birkin was filming Vadim's *Don Juan* with Brigitte Bardot, and finished after its release and the severe heart attack of May 1973.

So, yes, Jane Birkin claims this Venusian gift. And of course, it's obvious, Étienne Daho confirms: Jane has revealed the feminine side that Serge hid 'under a provocative cynicism and superficial misogyny.' For Serge, Jane was a permanent representation of the duality that needed exorcising. Much more than a mirror, she was the condition of his existence. She remembers the recording sessions for the pieces written for her after their breakup. 'At first, singing about the wounds one has caused seems like a terrible thing to do. Inside the recording booth, there was only one thing to do, to hit the highest notes I could, even if it meant breaking my voice, so that Serge shouldn't cry out of sadness, but for the beauty of the thing. I didn't think of it in these terms at the time, on that album, *Baby Alone in Babylone* [1983], and the successive ones, *Lost Song* [1987] and *Amours des feintes* [Love of Deceptions] [1990]: this triptych nurtured by our breakup, Serge gave me his feminine side to sing. He kept his provocative side for himself and explored it with his rasta experiences and songs like "The Boy": "*I'm the boy who can enjoy invisibility*", the only one I know that deals with homosexuality. By giving me his hurt side, he could keep doing his Gainsbarre.'

At their first meeting, Jane is a girl who already lives up to the later characterisation of her by Agnès Varda in her 1988 film *Jane B. for Agnès V.*: 'The encounter, on an assembly table, between a playful androgyne and a plasticine Eve.' Jane is insecure. 'I didn't have any breasts, I'd never appear on a *Playboy* centrefold, with the staple in the middle. What's more, I was married to John Barry, and that's all I was. I didn't like myself.' She finds some comfort in reading *Union Magazine*, which publishes letters written by 'girls like me': flat girls. But it's a blessing in disguise – breasts have always scared Lucien Ginsburg.

In 'Serge Gainsbourg, mort ou vices' (Serge Gainsbourg: dead or debauched), a falsely-posthumous interview with

Gainsbourg, conducted by Bruno Bayon for *Libération* in 1984, the question is asked – Serge, supposedly dead, projects himself from beyond the grave:

> – What do you invariably dislike and prefer in a woman? Apart from this basic misogyny.
> – … A big rack, that's what I can't stand. Mammary glands. I find them vile – but maybe that's the faggot in me: I like girls with small breasts … Big tits are a pain in the arse.

Gainsbourg (at his most trashy, decadent Gainsbarre) adds that he loathes 'pubic hair that goes all the way up to the navel.' A furry bush is disgusting, but he does want just a bit of hair. 'Maybe that's because I'm beardless. I mean: I have a hairless chest. Maybe it's a projection of myself on the other.' A form of homosexuality, the two of them conclude. Gainsbourg: 'Yeah, I like a girl to look like a little boy.'

What follows is a dialogue that would nowadays be banned, about the smell of redheads, unfuckable 'chunks' and blacks: 'I'm not very negrophile, either; that smells, smells from afar, "a negress possessed by the demon" – that's a quote from Mallarmé.' Gainsbourg then embarks on a eulogy of legs, 'anything but the Hottentot Venus! Legs have to be like a Rolls.'

If there is a magnificent body, it must be that of Mantegna's *Saint Sebastian*, 'a kind of orgasm in suffering. It's unfathomable, there is a sexual approach … Sexuality meets mysticism – the mystic …' In the 15th century, Mantegna paints three pictures of Saint Sebastian, the protector from the plague. The perfect body is bound, riddled with arrows from head to toe. Painted in 1490, the *Saint Sebastian* of Venice, the most despondent of the three, has the inscription: '*Nihili nisi divinum stabile est. Cœtera fumus*' (Nothing is permanent that is not divine. All else is smoke). Faced with life's transience: man, woman, what difference does it make?

'Gainsbourg was a woman,' according to the comics artist Joann Sfar, director of the film *Gainsbourg: A Heroic Life*. A prude who switches off the light to make love, a romantic who passionately reads *Lolita*, the scandalous novel published in 1955 by another Russian, Vladimir Nabokov.

And I shall be dumped where the weed decays / And the rest is rust and stardust.

These are the last two verses of the novel that Gainsbourg wanted to put to music, but he couldn't, because Stanley Kubrick, who had adapted it for the cinema in 1962, owned the rights. In 1980, Gainsbourg writes *Evguénie Sokolov*, a tale that portrays an artist who paints his own farts, powerful seismic waves that, captured in 'gasograms', sell at exorbitant prices. Moreover, the hero of the story is a paedophile. The title, published by Gallimard, is 'indexed between the two pansies Gide and Genet,' Gainsbarre bragged on Thierry Ardisson's show.

In 1971, Serge Gainsbourg releases *Histoire de Melody Nelson*, developed in London with the composer and arranger Jean-Claude Vannier. This short rock-opera sublimates a very young girl with red hair, an adorable tomboy, struck on her bike by Serge Gainsbourg's 1910 Rolls-Royce Silver Ghost. What follows is a romance, and a tragedy. In a continuation of *Slogan*, the man is getting on, while she is in the fresh bloom of youth – Melody isn't yet fifteen. Jane, who is ten years older, adapts her voice and appearance to the role of nymphet. 'Jean-Claude Vannier has said that Serge had always thought of himself as an old man. It's true, he was delighted to be seen with younger woman. Girl or boy didn't make that much a difference, he pictured himself as Dirk Bogarde in *Death in Venice*. In the holiday movies my parents took, I really look like a boy. And he loved my body. I didn't have Melody Nelson's age – fourteen autumns and fifteen summers – but I easily looked the part.'

The cover of the record is telling: Birkin's jeans are patched, they are 'sailor trousers', the photographer Tony Frank remembers. She is topless. And because she is pregnant with Charlotte, she holds a toy monkey to her stomach, 'Munkey, my uncle Mike won it in a pub raffle and gave it to me when I was a child,' she tells Ludovic Perrin, for *Le Monde*. Tony Frank designs a blue backdrop, luminous 'Melody' blue.

On 23 April 1970, at the Marble Arch Studio, Serge Gainsbourg is late. Jane is worried, 'she's almost in tears,' Tony Frank remembers. Then he arrives with a box: 'it's a *Carita* wig he's just bought,' short red hair. Gainsbourg is having fun. 'He loved to laugh,' says Tony Frank, who is also the creator of the cover that shows Michel Polnareff, wearing a cheesy pink 'fairy-tale princess' hat while exposing his backside. Gainsbourg plays, wearing the wig. He loved to masquerade as a girl.

If psychoanalyst Jacques Lacan's dictum that 'For each man, a woman is a symptom' holds true, Jane Birkin reveals a discrepancy in the definition of femininity. In 1978, Gainsbourg writes for his friend Régine:

> Women, that's a bit gay, quite effeminate / So effemi-nate, it's really queer / Women, they wear skirts / But what really irks / Women they wear stockings / Nylon or silk.

He's in love with Jane, whose appearance is androgynous. 'He sketched my breast, just a line with a tip. He said I was half-boy, half-girl, which he loved. He told me I looked like a Lucas Cranach painting and I was very flattered.'

Serge photographed in 1960.

thirteen

The twin

••

*G*ainsbourg lives with his double. On the cover of *Love on the Beat*, photographed by William Klein, he's made up like a woman – 'the spitting image of his sister'. Not Jacqueline, Jane Birkin points out: the other one. The twin. The unknown one, the one who never spoke, never featured in the magazines. She appears in a painting that escaped Lucien Ginsburg's ransacking of his own work in 1958. The small picture shows two children: 'my little sister and me, playing in the sand,' in a post-impressionist style, in the manner of Pierre Bonnard. Sand rake, polka dot sweater, he's tenderly leaning towards her with his legs tucked under. Everything is calm and captivating. The girl looks like a frog, a small, folded creature, her head bent.

Juliette Gréco has inherited this very intimate painting. Serge gave it to her when she performed 'La Javanaise'. 'They're in a public park, maybe in a sand pit. In the background, there's some greenery, a tree,' says Gréco, the *grande doyenne* confined to retirement since the stroke she suffered in 2016. 'A monochrome, 50×35 centimetres. A cherished possession. Blond hair, red hair. Gainsbourg was very feminine, fragile. At the time he was influenced by his wife [Élisabeth Levitzky]. The girl in the picture is ugly, his twin sister, she was Gainsbourg, as a woman, which was worse. She was hideous, ghastly. He wasn't ugly, he had an incredible inner beauty and irresistible charm.'

Serge and Liliane, an oddity: there is no acknowledged connection, each one is in their own bubble. At the end of her childhood, Liliane fades away. She could 'shoot her mouth off' publicly – scratch at the surface of the legend. But she under-stands quickly that celebrity is out of bounds. The older sister, Jacqueline, appears extensively in the biographies, in family or official photos, but the twin is remote. She is not against this occultation. She is elsewhere; contact with her brother becomes 'somewhat impersonal, he impressed me, because he could be quite aloof at times, there was a certain showmanship. He made me come to his place to admire his fabulously-designed interior,' she tells Gilles Verlant. In 1985, on the day of their mother's death, Serge, in tears, withdraws to Rue de Verneuil with Liliane. They listen to Ravel's 'Pavane for a Dead Princess'. 'That gave me the shivers.'

At a very young age, Liliane disappears from the fam-ily's radar. She is twenty when she becomes Madame Zaoui and moves to Casablanca with her husband. A mother of two, she teaches English. Serge, Jane and the children come by from time to time. 'Liliane moved away very early, I'm not sure if this wasn't unfair.' Jane Birkin fully understands. Her younger sister, Linda, has made her life 'without the slightest acknowledgement of the world of show business – otherwise it's suffocating. She married someone who has no notion of it whatsoever, she has three daughters, she has become a sculptress. My parents were very strong reference points: I went to France, because my mother, an actress, could no longer criticise me for speaking French badly, for example, because she didn't speak it herself. I was carefree. My films weren't shown in England, I complained a bit, but in fact it suited me very well. I was free here, like Liliane in Casablanca.'

There's more. The Ginsburgs had had a first son, Marcel, who died of pneumonia at the age of sixteen months. In 1927, after Jacqueline's birth, Olga is once more pregnant. It's a no. She consults an abortionist doctor, but, according to Gainsbourg's account of the miracle, she's put off by the chipped enamel bowl, the sluggishness of the place and the lack of hygiene. On 2 April 1928, she gives birth to twins. Liliane is born first. Jane explains: 'Olga's son has died, Jacqueline was born three years previously and now she expects twins. She doesn't dare to abort at Pigalle, and when the twins come out, it's Liliane first. Thinking that twins are always identical, she starts to cry, because she thinks she'll have three daughters! And when Serge appears, it's: a boy – joy and surprise! What a relief! Of course, Olga was prejudiced in a way that's typical of Jewish, oriental families, and also, in fact, of English ones.'

The stakes, however, are high. Serge fills the void left by the dead brother. He has to be perfect, he's not entitled to make a mistake. Jacqueline, the father's favourite, straightens out the omissions of the younger brother, buys the Mother's Day presents, makes sure everything is in order. Liliane finds herself suffocating, faced with a firm mother and a father who beats his children when they fail at their piano exercises, and then apologises in the evening.

'If one has, like me, a soul that's all twisted like a foetus, one needs to provoke in order to untangle it,' said Gainsbourg-Gainsbarre, Lucien-Serge, in search of an identity. The twins, even though fraternal, have a particular, dual, function. In search of their lost oneness, they occasionally confuse their genders. Thus, Liliane Ginsburg is the hidden part of her twin – the one who was called Ginette at school because he was so sweet. He told Gilles Verlant the story: 'Hey, Ginette, how are you, Ginette? One day, with my mother, I go to the greengrocer and, as it was raining, I put on my hood. And guess what the grocer did? She bent down and said: "And what would you like, young lady?" Ooooh … I was mortified. At least I was cute, and then it got worse.' He grows two 'big ears and that nose …'

The psychoanalyst René Zazzo, co-author, with Michel Tournier, of *The Paradox of Twins*, asserts that twins are not each other's double. 'Whatever the claims of creation myths, they do not form a pair: they form a couple, which is to say, a more or less stable distribution of tasks, of daily activities.' A couple where both members are truly 'one' and where 'the personality of either member is reaffirmed through the other and in relation to the other.'

In some of the oldest cultures, from Greece to Africa, the twin was considered to be a man who brings along his visible double. 'They have been the representation of a hermaphrodism capable of autoreproduction, thus of embryonic bisexuality, coupled with primary narcissism,' the psychoanalyst continues.

Being twinned can shackle, enslave. Gainsbourg attempts to free himself. (According to 'La Chanson du forçat' [The Song of the Condemned], written in 1967, which has become the theme song of the television series *Vidocq*):

He who has never let himself be shackled / Will never know freedom / I do, I know. I am an escapee.

Being a twin implies a fundamental duality that Gainsbourg will attempt to escape. In vain. Staying in an actors' premises, Serge, then married to Élisabeth Levitzky, found a discrete opening in a wardrobe. The closet gave access to a former Anglican church where performers and a jazz band came to rehearse. Lucien peeps. In 1991, the ex-wife tells the weekly *Elle*: 'The wardrobe was like a darkroom where the "negative" of Lulu was developed and one evening, in bright light, we saw the photograph: someone we didn't know, we, his best friends I, his wife. That wardrobe was like a dark belly, bathed in music, where Lucien Ginsburg curled up in a foetal position and from where he reappeared in a second birth under the name of Serge Gainsbourg.'

The release? That will be Jane: actress and actress' daughter, for a period of twelve years. Jane is not a twin, but she has a brother who is twelve months older. She has a twin's relationship with Andrew. 'What kind of child were you when you were seven?', the television critic Henri Chapier asks her in 1984, the day after the immense scandal caused by *The Pirate* at the Cannes Film Festival. The film is booed from the opening credits, the audience sings the advertising jingle for 'Dim' stockings whenever Jane embraces her female lover. 'I admired Andrew, my little soldier.'

She tries to resemble him. She cuts her hair. At boarding school, the others tease her: she's neither a girl, nor a boy, so what is she? 'At sixteen,' she admits to *Elle* in 1993, 'I still didn't have my period. My mother worried and dragged me to the doctor. Maybe I unconsciously delayed my puberty to better resemble my brother.' Later on, at sixteen, she is invited to a ball. She has just left boarding school on the Isle of Wight, where she has started a passionate relationship with one of the other girls. Her father dressed her like a girl and gave her a bunch of flowers. Andrew is at the bottom of the stairs and, looking at her, shouts out: 'It's over.' It will never be over. Andrew will never cease to follow in Jane's wake, he even plays her husband in *The Pirate*. Andrew is born exactly a year before Jane, in December; he on the 9th, she on the 14th. He witnesses Jane's transformation. She is born prematurely: frail, weepy, fearful and cold, and will turn into an optimistic woman with an easy laugh, who is able to let herself be sodomised, unfazed, on film, play the ingénue, sleep with Bardot under the eyes of men, and love Serge for who he really is. With his beard, his Repettos, his bling.

Portrait of Serge taken for the cover of the LP *Love on the Beat*.
© 1984 WILLIAM KLEIN

fourteen

Drag queens and company

•••

*A*ndrogynous ambiguity has always inspired Gainsbourg. In 1983, he writes:

> A feminine male / Slightly wild / A bit too feline / You
> know that you are / Hot, yes, like Bowie,

for Isabelle Adjani. He asks Jane to sing like a choirboy, in a very high voice. In 1971, he creates the song 'La Décadanse' (Decadance) for her. 'The idea was, after 300 years of face-to-face, to turn one's partner around. That was convenient, but, more importantly, very exhibitionistic. A man shows off his wife to the woman who is opposite him and who in turn is held by her husband,' Jane explains with astonishing innocence. It's a reversal.

With his father Joseph, a classical pianist resigned to the world of entertainment, the young Lucien Ginsburg discovers the grey areas of gender and sexuality. Joseph plays in transvestite clubs, notably at *Madame Arthur*, where he accompanies the stars of the genre, Coccinelle and Bambi. 'I went back there many times with him and my father, whom Serge adored. The transvestites called him Serjou and kissed him on the head,' Jane Birkin remembers. In 1946, the cabaret club *Madame Arthur*, a reference to the famous song by Paul de Kock, took over from the *Divan japonais*, established in 1890, where Yvette Guilbert had shot to fame.

In post-war Paris, Monsieur Marcel and Madame Germaine hold the reins of the establishment and know how to command respect. On stage, there is a small orchestra. Percussion, saxophone, bass and, on the piano, Joseph Ginsburg.

The show starts at 11pm and continues into the morning hours. Artistes, burlesque players and transvestites performed in tableaux separated by intervals. There is dancing here, but not among men. If this occurs, the orchestra stops: the establishment would risk being closed down by the authorities for infringing public decency, which was still strictly controlled at the time.

In 1954 Joseph, the father, is replaced by Lucien, the son, who plays there for two seasons. Nicknamed 'Père Jo', Joseph Ginsburg wasn't very funny on stage. 'When he moved, he looked more like an undertaker,' Louis Laibe, artistic director of *Madame Arthur* claimed. His son doesn't seem too different, dressed in a black tie, or navy-blue cross twill suit. 'The night is his domain: he always approaches it impeccably dapper. Like a poor gigolo pretending to be rich,' writes Yves Salgues.

Lucien, who is a painter, has no particular love for this kind of light musical entertainment. And yet, he develops the pieces of the show *Arthur Circus* with Louis Laibe, and registers their intellectual property rights in 1955. 'At *Madame*

Arthur, we were never shocking, or smutty: our premise was to gloss over the slightly deviant side of the whole thing by emphasising the allure of the performance,' Louis Laibe tells Gilles Verlant. 'One had to be very careful, in those days, if one didn't want to end up at the "Pointed Tower" [the Judicial Police at the Quai des Orfèvres], or to get beaten up at the exit. I quickly had the idea of writing the songs for our new show with Lucien. Its theme was the circus, which was a big part of what we did. After all, there were 35 performers on stage at the time, the venue was small, but our shows were famous all over the world! "Arthur Circus" was the opening number, then there was "La Trapéziste" [The Trapeze Artist], written in memory of a star from the Medrano circus, who'd had an accident.' And then there is 'Zita la Panthère' (Zita the Panther).

The first performers of Gainsbourg's music are unique characters: Maslowa, Toinou Coste, a lad of 120 kilos, who impersonated Fréhel, and 'Lucky Sarcelle, a former sidekick of Mistinguett,* who'd been fired from the *Folies Bergère* after missing his cue to go onstage, because he was snorting coke under the stairs. He was no oil painting, but he had nice legs: I presented him as "the only singer to sing with her legs"…' It was Lucky Sarcelle who performed 'Antoine le casseur' (Antoine the Scrapper), the first lyrics that were written by Gainsbourg, under the pseudonym of Julien Grix:

---

* Mistinguett was a singer and actress, who entertained at the *Folies Bergère* and the *Moulin Rouge* – at one time the highest-paid female entertainer in the world.

It's for him that I walk the streets / That I sell my rump and all the rest / And if he's a hot stallion / Then I'm a hot filly, too / The dunces I sponge from leave me quite cold / Only Antoine can get under my skin / My affection is so deep / That there's none but him that could reach its depth.

Two transgender pioneers performed at *Madame Arthur*'s: Coccinelle and Bambi. Bambi is Marie-Pierre Pruvot, born in Algeria as Jean-Pierre Pruvot. She became a woman, an artist, then a French teacher. She describes the trailblazers of the place in her memoirs, *J'inventais ma vie* (I Have Been Inventing My Life): Maslowa, in pink satin pajamas, is at the reception; he 'didn't wear a wig, and with his naturally blond hair, managed to create a somewhat feminine hairdo. He was always made up, but only slightly: he had very little stubble. His lips were drawn in a heart shape, like in 1925. What drew most attention, and even caused stares, were his eyes. Huge green eyes that could take on any expression, from innocence to malice, from tenderness to wrath, from admiration to mockery.' Maslowa had a self-deprecating sense of humour, she invented 'the persona of a dizzy young woman, both extravagant and good-natured' for herself.

Leaving *Madame Arthur* for the resort casinos or *Milord l'Arsouille*, Gainsbourg harbours a Slav sense of nostalgia. His fingers stained with nicotine, he who belonged, in his own words, 'to the royal plebs of Montmartre sidewalks' played 'My Man', in Billy Holliday's version, with hermaphroditic sensuality. But his father had lectured Lucien on the question of homosexuality. 'I never saw Gainsbourg go out with a tranny or a poof at the time,' Louis Laibe continues. 'That's why I was flabbergasted a few years later, when I saw him sing "Mon Legionnaire" [My Legionnaire],' a song performed by Dubas in 1936, and covered in 1987 by the Gainsbarre of *You're Under Arrest* – the music video is openly gay.

When it comes to homosexuality, Gainsbourg's case proves to be less than clear. Yes, Serge must have 'tried'. Jane Birkin is unfazed. If she weren't, she would be contradicting herself, and the ideas she had defended when demonstrating in support of marriage equality, as proposed by François Hollande's government in 2012. 'I find that the feeling of love has neither limits, nor fixed criteria.'

As a child, he was girlish. 'I was cute as a boy, not hideous. The guys fell in love, and I didn't understand what they wanted ... They wanted me to come home with them ... To take me with them to penetrate me ... This was about me acting the girl. I didn't understand,' he confides to Bayon in his 1984 'posthumous' interview for *Libération*. 'I have fucked guys,' he continues, 'all my life. I regretted having missed out on men when I was younger, and that they missed out on me. Missing out on them in terms of love. Because I have known some – they were good-looking lads – but then I was very prudish, so it simply didn't work. It didn't work, it didn't make sense. I guess that's a life I missed out on.' Who acts the guy, who the girl? Who is the sheath, the knife, the anvil?

fifteen

Of dogs and girls

....

*J*ane and Serge have never been separated. On 14 December 2016, Jane Birkin is 70. She is about to open a new chapter in a romantic and literary cycle that is built around her late companion. The concert and the accompanying record are entitled *Gainsbourg: le symphonique*: 24 songs with a classical arrangement by Nobu (the Japanese arranger and pianist Nobuyuki Nakajima), whom she met at a concert given in Japan for the victims of Fukushima.

Jane Birkin is particularly attached to Japan, which is sophisticated, polished, creative and in love with French *chanson*. In 2011, she donates the €111,000 she made through the sale at auction of the prototype 'Birkin' Hermès handbag to the associations of victims of Fukushima. She, for her part, had been given it by the luxury brand she will soon leave. In June 2015, a shiny fuchsia 'Diamond Birkin 35' in *porosus* crocodile is sold for €202,000 by Christie's Hong Kong. Not comfortable

(opposite) Jane, Serge and his beloved bulldog bitch Nana, photographed at home in the Rue de Verneuil, Paris.
(PHOTO BY PICOT/GAMMA-RAPHO VIA GETTY IMAGES)

with the slaughtering conditions of the alligators used to produce the crocodile skin models, Jane Birkin orders Hermès to
rename the bag. She won't be an accomplice to the murder of
animals. But at Hermès, the waiting list for acquiring a 'Birkin
bag' still extends to several years. The Birkin look is legendary.
Ultra-short dresses of the *baby doll* period, black for the night,
beaded for the shoot, floral for the summer. The muse of the
sixties also wears platform shoes with elegant flared jeans.

In Normandy, at the Trouville jetty, *Promenade des Anglais*,
she sports her flared 'elephant leg' jeans, enhanced by romantic
blouses. Then, as the 2000s approach, we see her dressed by
Burberry, in a trench coat – a military gabardine that women
have discovered for themselves – and Converse, a 'grunge'
brand she comes to represent. Her daughters resemble her.
Charlotte, a melancholic elf refusing to grow up and Lou, the
rebel, irritated by celebrity.

To perform *Gainsbourg: le symphonique*, another magnificent gift offered to Serge in 2017, she wears a black smoking
jacket – the famous evening wear designed by Yves Saint
Laurent in 1966 – shifting it from the masculine to the feminine.
In 2016, the fashion house's creative director, Hedi Slimane,
chose Jane to renew this centrepiece of the Saint Laurent style.
She wears it loose, with black boots or sometimes white trainers
and a pristine white blouse. She is extremely elegant, slender
and gracious.

This orchestral reinterpretation of Gainsbourg, designed
to flatter the 'classical' composer inside Gainsbourg, is magnificent. It is pure emotion. It seduces audiences who give her

standing ovations from Japan to the US. She is surprised, says that Serge was just this: the manifestation of genius. But without her?

Why does she find it so difficult to claim her part of this triumph? For this 'Gainsbourg Symphonique', as always, she refers to her men: Serge, obviously, Philippe Lerichomme, the man in the background who watches over all things Gainsbourg since 1975: publication, republication, remixes, archives, curios, good ideas … and here, Nobu, the arranger. She allows them to reap the applause, while she illuminates the stage with an aura of grace – and it's clear what she is trying to say.

Gripers may object that Jane has already done it all: Gainsbourg with oriental sauce in *Arabesque*, 'Gainsbourg: the lyrics', read with Michel Piccoli and Hervé Pierre at the Théâtre de l'Odéon, and now 'she feeds us' Gainsbourg with violins. It is true that this creative form is new. There is no other example of it the world over. If the music of Astor Piazzolla or Antônio Carlos Jobim, two legends of the 20th century, has been rearranged in every thinkable way, their successive spouses took no part in this. 'A beautiful couple like this one, which brings together a composer and a performer – we don't know of another one like this,' Juliette Gréco comments.

The same naysayers have also rejected *À la légère*, *Rendez-vous*, *Fictions* and *Enfants d'hiver*, Jane Birkin's last four albums, either written by her or her singer friends – from Alain Souchon to Gérard Manset, from Françoise Hardy to Zazie – or put together from cover versions chosen with impeccable taste – Neil Young, The Divine Comedy, Caetano Veloso, Kate Bush.

What do people want? For Jane and Serge to live on. Jane has understood this unconscious, visceral desire. She has decided: enough with the worries, out with the trash. With humour, elegance and patience, she will carry the burden of Saint Lucien of Antioch, who believed in the humanity of Christ, and who metamorphosed by his own volition into Saint Serge, the orthodox, medieval hero of the Russian nation. The whiners will say: what commercial opportunism! They'll say that in the same way they saw it in the contemporary artist Yoko Ono, the grave-digger of the Beatles: in bad faith.

There is no denial from Birkin. Serge Gainsbourg was no angel, she has even travelled into the darkest parts of the night with him. He pushed her to the extreme, but she knew how to protect herself from the flames of hell, because she is an artist, and an actress. And he was, she repeats, 'funny, immensely funny.' When Birkin wants to explain something, she goes beyond the question. She talks about the songs, the characters, her father, her mother, her children, and Serge. She mentions those close to her, and her partners, by their first name: Philippe, Charlotte, Andrew, Anno, Étienne, Gabrielle, Emmanuel, Olivier … one has to keep up. The same goes for places: from the Finistère to London, via Normandy and the Rue de Verneuil.

In Paris, she now lives close to the Museum of Natural History. She has a garden. The interior houses an inviting labyrinth of photographs, wall hangings, saucepans, gilding, posters, flowers, kitsch, drawings, art, of seemingly everything, all of it displayed against the austerity of black walls. There is a strange temporal continuation here, of which the family constitutes a focal point that is both immutable and fluctuating, with its copper saucepans and king-size stoves.

With Jane Birkin, everything is in motion, in tiny ripples. She is not pretentious, she is chic. We have been acquainted with her new dog, a bulldog that eats the visitor's shoelaces with persistence. At the time of her relationship with Gainsbourg, there was Nana, a bullterrier that looked like Serge as a girl, big tapered ears and a pointy snout. In the drawing room at Rue de Verneuil, 'where everything fossilised at the death of his mother, Olga, in 1985, Gainsbourg had kept the dog's special place,' the journalist Bruno Bayon relates. No one could sit down in it, and any who did so was sternly ousted. The fussiness, already pronounced when he lived with Jane, increased over time.

Nana, the English bullterrier, was an old dream of his. One day, Gainsbourg bumped into a man and his bullterrier at a restaurant. He 'thought he saw a medieval tapestry,' he told the journalists of *30 Millions d'amis* (30 Million Friends), who had come to film his games with Nana. 'And I said to myself that once I had a garden and a house, I'd have a dog like this one. Jane heard of this and gave me one, bought in London,' because the 'poor' French only liked poodles. 'As soon as we cross the Channel, the way people look at this beautiful bullterrier changes: "What is this thing? A sheep, a pig?"'

The hidden beauty of the ugly / Reveals itself sooner rather than later, sings Gainsbourg in 1979.

> Same music, same reggae for my dog / That everyone
> found so ugly / Poor pooch it's me who drinks / And it's
> him that died of cirrhosis / Must have been by osmosis /
> That's how much he lapped up whatever I said.

To the hideous, God must extend some of His mercy.

Nana is all white, apart from the ears, which are brown.
One day, in Spain, she disappears from a hotel. So Gainsbourg,
every bit as upset as when his father died, agrees to take part in
a television programme with a huge audience, on the condition
that the host talks neither about him, nor about Jane, but about
the dog. Nana reappears, covered in ticks and scars. Nana, the
animal of happy days, of trips to the countryside, of outdoor
family lunches at Cresseveuille. When Nana dies, Gainsbourg
is in tears. It announces the end of a world.

'You know,' Gainsbourg says on *30 Millions d'amis*, 'the
people who walk their dogs, let me tell you, it's not the dog
who is being taken out on the leash, it's the master.' It is said
that master and dog resemble each other. This assertion was
reaffirmed in the most romantic film of the time (the sixties)
Un Homme et une Femme. The director Claude Lelouch points
his camera at the Deauville promenade during sunset and films
the evening stroll of the owners and their dogs, melting into one
single silhouette. But, in 1965, the bossa-nova and the caresses of
Jean-Louis Trintignant and Anouk Aimée aren't really doing
it for Jane. There are within the Serge version of Birkin deep

fissures that are hardly compatible with the romantic swaying of composer Pierre Barouh's 'Chabadabada', or with the sprint of a whippet on the Deauville beach. The image of a whippet, alert and lithe, would, of course, fit Jane Birkin like a glove: all vertical lines and restraint. Too simple.

What does it for this fragile Englishwoman is the English bulldog, a chubby watchdog with square paws and excessively-drooping jowls. When turning the page on her relationship with Serge, she initiates the series of bulldogs. Betty, a gift from her new companion, the filmmaker Jacques Doillon, and then ill-tempered Dora. Today it's Dolly: adolescent, cheerful and carefree, even as Jane deals with the tragedy of her older daughter Kate's death, and is impeded, but not reduced, by grief.

Jane with her daughters and bulldogs, that's a hall of mirrors, of distorting reflections. The English bulldog is as thickset as she is longilineal and delicate. It farts, at times in bursts, as befits the breed. For years, she has been making apologies to others while trying to contain the odours. Birkin is chic, she has style, could be smooth, but she multiplies the vital signs without excluding what's animal.

Through her affection for bulldogs, Jane is very much a part of old England. Since the 13th century, this beast, like his cousin the bullterrier, engaged in battles with nature, the dog fighting the bull. It almost disappeared when bullbaiting was prohibited in 1835. An enthusiast recreated the breed, bending the curve of violence to the point of transforming it into overflowing tenderness and demonstrable laziness. Some found it ugly. 'Coquetry brought bulldogs into my life,' Jane Birkin

laughs. 'They're a capricious breed: they have difficulty breathing, problems with their eyes, their skin ... but they are animals
that make people in the streets laugh, that amuse children in
parks, and that alone, that's already pretty great.'

The new recruit to the Birkin family spreads out on her
back, drools remorselessly and affirms her tendency to flatu-
lence. Jane drinks tea and continues: that is something else
she loved in Serge, his ability to talk about 'loud ones', then
of metaphysics, in the manner of Raymond Queneau's Zazie.*
'He wrote "Exercice en forme de Z" [Exercise in the Form of
a Z], for example [Jane hums, at great speed, with vacant eyes]:

> Zazie / On her visit to the zoo / Zazie sucking on her
> Zan / Had fun with a brilliant verse / By Isidore Isou,
> when – bang! / A blizzard wind / Blows from her trou-
> ser / There they zig-zag in the air / Zazie and her blazer.

Who, other than Gainsbourg, she asks, could mix Zan,** wind
and Isou, the founder of the Lettrist movement together in this
way? Who, other than Gainsbourg, could have taken her to
such depths of desire?

In the famous 1981 'post-mortem' interview, granted in his
lifetime to Bruno Bayon for *Libération*, Gainsbourg imagined
himself, having departed from this life, hidden in a very special

---

* Eponymous hero of Queneau's 1959 novel *Zazie dans le Métro*, filmed
for the big screen by Louis Malle in 1960.

** A make of liquorice.

place: the inside of a dog. 'There are gases. Flammable gases. So, I light ... a match.' To see the dog's intestines, he explains. 'Since he'd been inside my head in my lifetime, I decided to go into his belly ... I take a look through the hole ...', Gainsbourg explains, before adding: 'The eye was in the anus and it looked at Cain ...',* the rival, murderous brother of Abel, son of Adam and Eve. The good, the bad, the forbidden, and the hand of the Almighty that crushes the drunk, and the guzzler's fist that takes revenge on innocence. All these dark places! Bruno Bayon jumps on the Gainsbourg train at a time when it had already entered the endless tunnel of 'gainsbarrian' decadence. He hangs out at Rue de Verneuil until the bitter end of Serge Gainsbourg, who's become 'a reclusive old man who plays the fool, the roughneck, an old boy locked into the grave of obsessions,' even as he had married Bambou: 'androgyne of angular appearance, the promise of youth'. One day, Bayon finds himself lying on the host's bed to attend a screening of a particular kind. 'On one side, he'd filmed his encounter with Screamin' Jay Hawkins,' the American bluesman with whom he had sung 'Constipation Blues' on television in 1983, one of them adding constipated onomatopoeias, the other translating: 'he has pooped.' Backstage, 'it was a riot, he was blotto, he didn't speak a word of English,' Bayon remembers.

He simultaneously shows the intrepid and aghast journalist a pornographic film of the worst variety, a tape of bestiality

---

* From: Bruno Bayon, *Serge Gainsbourg raconte sa mort*, (Serge Gainsbourg Relates his Death) Grasset, 2001.

where the anal rape of a very young girl by a dog is set up. That's the point where 'the heart fails,' it's 'like Georges Bataille,'* Bayon adds. 'At the same time, it's a cosy nook, a moment of simple camaraderie, intimate, harmonious with Bambou who is there, and Serge who is in stitches and repeats: "Look at that, she's crying for real,"' as if these sobs were the ultimate moment of life.

Pushing his audience to the limit, declaring very casually: 'Let's say that for the woman, I am a necessary evil and, for me, she is damaged goods.' Calling the young Catherine Ringer, who openly admits on television that she has appeared in porn films, a whore. Insulting the American star Whitney Houston by hissing to her, on air: 'I want to fuck you,' in front of an appalled Michel Drucker, the guardian of Sunday-afternoon propriety. Gainsbourg is having a blast, Jane, voluntarily absent, remains silent. '*Baiser* is the most beautiful [French] verb, I think, because it means kissing with the mouth, as well as fucking with the prick,' he explains to Bruno Bayon. 'One mustn't be afraid to say: "I fuck you, I fuck." I no longer make love, I fuck.'

We are not here to establish the boundaries between provocation, the sources of extreme eroticism, and reality. The artist sees both beauty and ugliness. He is sometimes punished for this, doomed to the flames of hell. 'Why do you always seek to know and reveal the vile within mortals?' asks the priest, cousin

* French intellectual who wrote extensively on eroticism, surrealism and transgression (Story of the Eye, Solar Anus, Erotism). His estranged wife Sylvia married Jacques Lacan, whose writing Bataille influenced.

of the murderess of men, in *Don Juan 73*. 'Why reveal to them their blemishes? That is where true sin lies, Jeanne … That's worse than a murder.'

The *chanson* may be a minor art, but it's a 'miner' art, the singer and songwriter Claude Nougaro pointed out, while sticking on his forehead the little lamp that miners use to explore the bowels of the earth, to find a foothold there. Gainsbourg, who copied everything with talent, emerges from street culture, transfigures the tradition of the *chanson réaliste* and of the *cabarets* of Montmartre, found along the old fortified city walls of Paris and the Place Clichy, at Barbès, as well as in Pigalle, his childhood home. Built to collect taxes at the gateway to the capital, the fortifications barred entry to the out-of-town population. They have become synonyms for the frontiers of wretchedness and the spread of prostitution. They were also the epicentres of public piss-ups, as Fréhel, Serge's idol, sings in 1938:

> What has become of the fortifications / And the li'l bistrots at the gates / That was the stage of all the chansons / Of the pretty songs of days gone by / Where are then Julot / Nini, Golden Cap / And beefy Li'l Louis / So famous back then / What has become of the fortifications / And all the heroes of the chansons?

Disappeared: replaced by 'six-storey buildings' with all the conveniences, the author Michel Vaucaire concludes. The '*pierreuses*', who work the street on behalf of their pimp, hang around at the gates.

French *chanson* wasn't always as prudish as it was in the paradoxically moderate post-war years. If we get irritated today by trashy rap lyrics, we only have to remember the *café-concert* of the 19th century and the Roaring Twenties in the interwar period. One isn't in the least inhibited: the fringe is the fringe, and the *bourgeoisie* slums it at the *Chat noir* or the *Divan japonais*. The *chanson réaliste*, of which Gainsbourg is one of the pop successors, reveals every perversity. Here we are in the shady underworld of the streetwalkers of the outer boulevards, of little girls and old men. Everything is exposed without any taboo, crudely, with its dose of despair and skullduggery. Thus in 'Sous le pont noir' (Under the Black Bridge) by Raoul Moretti-Lucienne Boyer, brilliantly performed by Fréhel in 1933, there are the men who go home with fourteen-year-old girls:

> But one can guess by their charms / That the months
> of the wet nurse don't count.

In *chanson* circles, such explicit titles as 'La Pierreuse consciencieuse' (The Conscientious Street Walker) for example, are popular:

> For fourteen cents, the hand in the pocket / Even under
> the eye of the cop who watches below / I polish the
> dart of the guy I hook / The hand in the pocket / For
> fourteen cents.

Serge Gainsbourg has often said that he had frequented the

brothels and prostitutes of Barbès when he was young. Desire, money, expenditure and avarice obviously have, in a Freudian sense, a strong link with sex. At the juncture between realism and *chanson de variété*, Édith Piaf, a child of the street, was brought up in a brothel that her grandmother ran in Bernay, in Normandy. The working girls were her friends, her nannies. In 1936, in the film *The Tomboy*, she takes on an issue that is parallel to that of prostitution: drug use, and the deprivation it causes:

> Everyday happiness / Really means nothing to me / Virtue is nothing but weakness / It sees its end in heaven / I prefer the promise / Of artificial paradise.

In his own way and by comparison, Gainsbourg is an idealist. He was not a follower of psychoanalysis. In *Le Divan* (The Couch), a television programme presented by Henri Chapier, in late 1989, the singer is ill-at-ease, tongue-tied, elliptic, mumbling, broken. 'I shoot myself to be reborn,' is his off-the-mark answer when the FR3 host asks him some questions about his inner demons. He sticks to a *leitmotif*: 'Create or die!' There can be no stagnation. The thousand and one shades of grey – dark grey – of Lucien Ginsburg were painted sky blue by Jane Birkin.

Jane, Régine and Serge ring in the new year at Régine's night club in Paris, in 1977.

(Photo by Bertrand Rindoff Petroff/Getty Images)

sixteen

Régine

....

'Belonging to Serge was complicated.' Thus speaks a central character in Serge and Jane's kaleidoscope: Régine. She sets the stage of passion, organises the conquest of celebrity as much as the furtive liaisons. When she first meets Gainsbourg in 1952, she is a barmaid at the *Whisky à Gogo*, Rue du Beaujolais, where the jet set convene to learn the cha-cha-cha. He is working as a pianist in the same street, at the cabaret *Milord l'Arsouille*, where Jean Yanne, dressed up as a priest, tells salacious anticlerical jokes. The 'casual elegance', the big ears, the short hair, the smooth gaze and the drooping eyelids of the author of the 'Poinçonneur des Lilas' fascinate her.

One night, Régine confesses that she finds him wonderful. 'He mumbled: "Don't exaggerate," as if asking for more.' Régine invites Serge to *Whisky à Gogo*, her bar. He goes into raptures over the turntables, is amazed that Régine herself plays the tunes. That way, she explains, there is no gap between the songs. She shows him the dance floor. 'He contemplates it and asks: "What do you call it?" – "Well, a discotheque." That's how the word was coined in 1955,' according to Régine's recollection.

The daughter of Polish Jews, born in Belgium in 1929, Régina Zylberberg moves to Paris after her father loses his bakery in Anderlecht, Belgium, at poker. Escaped to the *zone libre* during the war, she learns to sing and party while awaiting the return of her *papa*, who is gambling at the Aix-en-Provence casino.

After the liberation of France, she runs the café her father has opened in Paris. 'My childhood took place during the war; I already had to deal with problems that were more complicated than childhood. I was fifteen, I set up the terrace, I served cheesecakes. I thought it was great. It was a *café-salon*, a funny place with colourful customers,' she writes in *Me, My Stories*.

In 1947, the future 'Queen of the Night' marries Paul Rotcage. One night, he takes her to the *Bœuf sur le toit cabaret*, she sits far away, all the way up in the gods, where nothing ever happens. Then: 'I saw the breasts of Henri Salvador's wife. They were very beautiful and she showed them generously,' she continues. 'Never again,' she decides to herself, mapping out the VIP areas in her head. To further that goal, the pretty brunette, plump and endowed with a charming little lisp, opens *Chez Régine* in 1956. But it's at *New Jimmy's* that she introduces France to 'the twist'. Régine doesn't drink. Confessing to *Paris Match*, in January 2016, she says: 'I accidentally got wasted at my club, at *Jimmy's*. The Gypsy musicians were playing earsplittingly; vodka, which is the colour of water, was flowing in gushes and people were all over each other. I can't remember anything. I eventually found myself at home, completely naked in front of my fridge. My dress had gone. I've never known where I left it or, more importantly, who took it off me!' Drugs? No. 'Plenty of the clients took them, and quite heavily, too.' Régine doesn't mind her detractors, as long as she's talked about at all. She enjoys starting false rumours and she waits for their echo with glee. Régine doesn't like to sleep. Sleeping is a waste of time. She loves the night. She loves to dance and fool around. 'I took over a little club for 40 people, I danced the cha-cha-cha at Monte Carlo, and *voilà* ...'

'The *New Jimmy's* doesn't admit suburban plebs, but *le Tout-Paris*. A 50,000-franc membership fee and 18,000 francs for the bottle of whisky,' *Actualités* informs its viewers in 1965. What intrigues the journalist from French television is that the 'Queen of the Night' has competition, from a young American, James Arch, who has opened the *Bus Palladium* at Pigalle, for the suburbanites. It puts at their disposal shuttle buses for 2.00 francs. Salvador Dali goes there, so do the Beatles.

> At the Palladium, Pigalle-side, it's not quite London,
> but it's a ride,

sings Léo Ferré in 1966. And Gainsbourg in response:

> You like nitroglycerINe / At Bus Palladium it rings
> OUT / Rue Fontaine's a packed school / For the boys
> from Liverpool.

(from the song 'Qui est in, Qui est out' [Who Is In, Who Is Out]). 'Oh well,' Régine retorts, serene in a little black dress. 'James Arch's understanding of nightlife isn't very clear; after all, the night is full of pitfalls, and it's very hard,' she says, before mentioning her other rival, Madame Martini, a Russian-Polish woman who is married to a Syrian suspected of espionage, with whom she has acquired the *Folies Bergère* and a bundle of other nightclubs. In Paris, Hélène Martini has opened the Russian cabaret *Raspoutine*, decorated by her friend, the painter and sculptor Erté, who is one of the architects of the art deco style. She had previously asked him to design the costumes for her transvestite cabaret, the *Narcisse*. At the *Raspoutine*, Gainsbourg feels right at home.

Serge and Jane's first night of passion follows this well-trodden path: *New Jimmy's, Madame Arthur, Raspoutine.* Jane doesn't yet know what she's getting into, she is mesmerised. Régine will never disavow her friendship with Jane Gainsbourg. Nor her admiration for this young Englishwoman who wears see-through dresses with the same elegance and poise she displays in jeans and white trainers, who sits on the floor when others dine, who dances while the guests wallow in their ennui.

'I am a geisha,' Régine asserts to Thierry Ardisson in 2006, reeling off the list of her lovers: Robert Mitchum, Gene Kelly, Warren Beatty, Steve McQueen, Jean-Claude Killy, Björn Borg, Carlos Monzón, Jacques Brel or the matador El Cordobés. 'I'd seen him at Nîmes, embracing the bull – on his knees in front of it. He wanted to give me a dowry, to indemnify me, if I abandoned the night.' Omar Sharif, 'who was afraid of dogs, so this couldn't work out, since I had one.' Claude François: 'We danced together, made some moves, we'd already had an adventure together. I came up with his song "Belles! Belles! Belles!"

[originally an Everly Brothers song]. Then we had an intense affair: eight days in bed, without letting up.' And Françoise Sagan? 'I was eighteen, she was 24, we did everything together. If only I could have been a lesbian!'

Régine is not a lesbian. She loves men, but won't let anyone walk over her, she won't be tied naked to a radiator, and won't be made to defend sodomy. Her first love, a nephew of the Chief Rabbi of Lyon, promised to marry her when she was of age, but was taken to Auschwitz in 1943. She's not afraid.

At the beginning of the sixties, Gainsbourg is in search of voices. And Régine wants to sing. Charles Aznavour writes the song 'Nounours' (Teddy Bear) for her, he wants her to sing 'La Javanaise' to figure out her style, as well as music by Renée Lebas, a *réaliste* singer of Romanian Jewish extraction. Then they had the idea of calling Gainsbourg. First subject of their conversation: his producer, Émile Stern, author of a song that Serge loved. 'Tire, tire, tire l'aiguille' (Pull, Pull, Pull the Needle) is inspired by Ashkenazi folklore and he had given it to Renée Lebas. Finding herself 'too old to sing love songs', Lebas had ended her career to concentrate on promoting artists, among them Régine and the singer Serge Lama. 'The next day at three, I see Serge Gainsbourg accompanied by a young woman who has pulled out some knitting.' Régine, who knew him as a bohemian, now encounters him as a family man: he has married the very jealous Françoise Pancrazzi, known as 'Béatrice'. They have two children, Paul and Natacha.

To forestall any possibility of a domestic scene, Régine receives them in a dressing gown and curlers, 'the next time she didn't come back.' Gainsbourg sits down at the piano and hums the melody of: 'J'te prête Charlie mais il s'appelle reviens' (I'd Lend You Charlie, But his Name is 'Come Back'). 'I was sitting down, somewhat amazed; he explains the orchestration, the backing vocals. Then he pulls out a sheet of paper with some lines of text end I hear the beginning of "Laissez parler les p'tits papiers" [Let the Little Papers Talk] ... I instantly say to myself: that's my song. There was total silence. Stern, Lebas and I, we all look at each other at the same time, saying: "Fantastic."'

Serge Gainsbourg knows everything there is to know about French *chanson*. Marie Dubas is the creator of 'Mon légionnaire', by Marguerite Monnot and Raymond Asso. In 1987, Gainsbourg/Gainsbarre covers the song on *You're Under Arrest*, as if he wanted to emphasise that his first real encounter with *chanson* took place in the thirties, with the *réaliste* songs.

Régine's voice reminds him of Fréhel (1891–1951), the great *chanteuse réaliste* he had met by chance one day in 1938, in Rue Chaptal; she was prematurely worn out by drugs and alcohol. Régine and Serge share the same passion for Fréhel, considered more genuine than Piaf. They loved her tribulations; they were touched by her love for Maurice Chevalier (whom Mistinguett had enticed away from her). 'That was our sentimental side, as Parisian kids.'

'Les P'tits Papiers' was written in reference to 'P'tits Pavés', (Little Cobblestones) a hit in the early 20th century, and part of Fréhel's repertoire; he had also covered it himself. Gainsbourg wrote twelve songs for Régine; each time, he thought of Fréhel and strived for perfection. Régine is a singer in the *réaliste* tradition: she plays the game. But even she has her limits. 'One day I told him we couldn't bring her back to life, that's how angry I was!'

'His thing,' Régine explains to Bruno Bayon in 2006, for *Libération*, 'was to make me desire the song, in the way one desires a man. When I called him for an album, he'd weasel out of it, get lazy. It was an SM relationship. Serge wanted the desire to come from me, through my desire for the songs he wrote for me. He literally made me pine from the moment the ritual began.' Régine remembers one day when, at Rue de Verneuil, before offering her a new song, he asks her if she has seen *Scarface* by Brian De Palma. 'We climbed the stairs to his room, which is covered in black serge and contains a very low bed, covered in vicuña fur; he indicates a place for me: "Lie down." At first, I had some misgivings ...' A screen descends and the De Palma film begins. 'He took off his shoes (he takes great care of his things, folds everything neatly). "Look", he pronounced in his whispered voice, and I say to myself, hypocrite floozy, "What does he want? Is this a test?"' This is an interrogation in the course of which Gainsbourg asks her if she has the nerve to sing whatever it is he gives her, without revealing the title. 'After four hours, with him still wondering out loud whether to play it to me, he opens a notebook, writes something in it, puts it down on the piano: "I'm not telling you the title …" and begins to tinkle, like, badly. I must not move, must not breathe … "That's not the right sound for you, for you, it should be more like this …" And, finally, he goes: "*Women, that's a bit gay … That's very, very, very effeminate,*" looking sideways. I'm thinking: if I show him that I'm already thrilled, he'll think I'm an arse-licker …'

Gainsbourg attended all the recording sessions. He wears one down. He tries to exhaust his partner, to bring out the emotion he wants. He demands higher octaves, pushes the singer to the verge of tears. Threatens to reject her. Passionate, sexual, amorous, extreme.

On 20 January 1967, Régine is asked to interview her friend Gainsbourg for television. He keeps twisting his hands and mouth, He has a sticking plaster on his nose. 'I haven't seen you in four months, what have you done?' Régine asks. 'I hit a door in a gallery, where I went to buy an atrocious Dalí … I was travelling, there was an earthquake, I was blamed for a fire at a restaurant. In Yugoslavia, I lit a cigarette using a banknote.' Régine knows the real story, but doesn't let on; laughing, she sifts reality from dreams. Serge has spent nine weeks in Colombia where he filmed a flop, *The Looters*, by Jacques Besnard, co-starring Jean Seberg. He set fire to a restaurant by leaving behind a match that wasn't put out properly, and ends up at the police station. He hired the services of a

prostitute from the port of Cartagena, who joined him on set, he made friends with a little girl and gave her his record *L'Eau à la Bouche* (Mouthwatering). His wife, Béatrice Pancrazzi, from whom he is supposedly divorced, made him scenes. Régine knows that that's what Serge is like: a poet of truth.

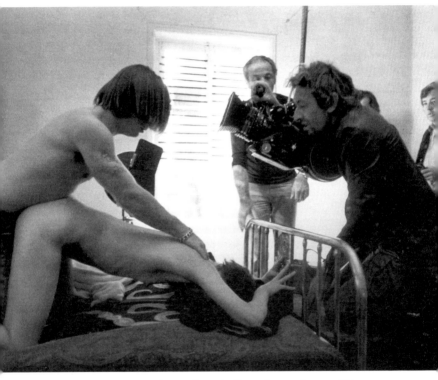

Serge directs Jane Birkin and Joe Dallesandro on the set of his
movie *Je t'aime moi non plus*, 1975.

(Photo: © Georges Pierre)

seventeen

Je t'aime moi non plus

. . . .

*I*f *Slogan* is the film of their encounter, the erotic tension between Jane and Serge is doubtless most candidly revealed in *Cannabis* (French Intrigue)*,* by Pierre Koralnik. Filmed in 1970, Koralnik's film imagines a particularly Gainsbourgian conundrum: a three-way relationship, one woman, two men – whereas the more common version of the fantasy is that of two women, one man. Serge Morgan (Gainsbourg) is a con-tract killer who works for the American mafia, assisted by his young accomplice, Paul (Paul Nicholas), an ephebe who has a passionate, but unrequited, desire for him. Serge meets Jane Swenson (Birkin) on an aeroplane and falls in love with her. An ambassador's daughter, she follows the two partners in crime into the chaos of score-settling between dealers. We're left with two castaways: he's wounded by gunshot, she's a skinny rich girl; both of them before Paul, who is dying of jealousy. The sex scenes are explicit, with close-ups of kissing lips, breasts being caressed. She mimes pleasure. He is tender.

The mixture between fiction and reality follows a common path once more: there's a gory scene at *Madame Arthur*, where Serge mows down the drag queens and fake Marilyns, with opium dens, steamy love in a car, naked admiration of the grand chandelier and Chagall ceiling at the Paris Opera. Serge dies in the end, killed by Paul. Jane screams. Previously, she had told him: 'We have been daydreaming: I knew with you that this wasn't possible. You have to attack us, you have to destroy: then you will be clean, you will be free.'

Serge Gainsbourg has his demons. He fends them off, dodges them: homosexuality, Jewishness, brotherhood. While working on *Je t'aime moi non plus*, he writes the album *Rock Around the Bunker*, a denunciation of the perfidies of Nazism, as well as the societies that have spawned and continue to harbour them. Violence is unheeding, it springs from the depths of humanity, it leads to the worst, like this Night of the Long Knives, the blood-soaked homosexual orgy of 1934 which is described, boogie-woogie style, in 'Nazi Rock'. It leads to 'Tata teutonne' (Teutonic Queen):

> Otto is a Teutonic Queen / Full of ticks and nits / Who sucks his own tits / while tickling his nipples,

and to abomination. Gainsbourg is Jewish, he has worn the yellow star and watches the 'SS in Uruguay' guzzle papaya juice under their straw hats.

Serge also wants to write an album for Jane; for lack of time, he delegates the lyrics to Philippe Labro. *Lolita Go Home* is released in 1975. The cover is a more modest reframing (without the naked chest) of a photograph published in *Lui* in December 1974. At the time, Francis Giacobetti, nicknamed

'Frank Gitty', captures Jane naked, in a suspender belt and high heels, handcuffed to a radiator or an iron bed, on a striped mattress. The trashy SM setting is designed by Serge. He writes a caption on the portfolio entitled 'Jane Érotojane': 'See how she suddenly perks up like Bartholdi's *Statue of Liberty*. Liberty, my foot, I tell her: in this dump, it's only ever the stockings that manage to get a run in ...' In a second part, a pretext for some fashion spread, a dispute ensues. The woman is pulled by her hair, beaten. At the time, elegance allowed for the taking of considerable liberties.

Serge's first film, *Je t'aime moi non plus*, is released in 1976. The Carpentiers, Maritie and Gilbert, big shots of Saturday-night prime-time television, play the role of his intermediaries with Jacques-Éric Strauss, who ends up commissioning the film from Gainsbourg. The subject is up to him, it's only the title that is insisted upon by the producers, Jacques-Éric Strauss and Claude Berri, with a view to capitalising on the global success of the 1968 song.

Are the Carpentiers happy to champion a polemic feature that deals with homosexual desire, gender and sodomy? They perform a sort of 'great balancing act', says Frédéric Bonnaud, director of the *Cinémathèque Française*. 'A paradox in the image of Jane and Serge.' Jane – with short hair, a tank top, jeans and a dangling belt – plays Johnny, a waitress in a roadside bar somewhere in the American desert. She gets her nickname from her almost non-existent breasts, and from her arse. In French cinema, Jane is an eroticised, exquisite body, discovered via the character of Pénélope in Jaques Deray's *The Swimming Pool*.

Johnny/Jane is seduced by the charm of a homosexual truck driver, Krassky, alias Krass, played by Joe Dallesandro, an actor who is close to Andy Warhol and the Factory. He is the muse of the filmmaker Paul Morrissey, who hires him for his trilogy *Flesh*, *Trash*, *Heat*. And, because he is the iconic sex symbol of American underground cinema, Gainsbourg wants him for his strange film.

The American actor, atrociously dubbed in French, plays a brawny macho with a steely gaze. He wears belts with a buckle that we hear him undo, drives a knackered heavy tipper truck – a Mack painted in a murky yellow and adorned with a pin-up figurine, a freebee from Veedol lubricants. Krass has a lover, the tortured introvert Padovan (Hugues Quester), who keeps fiddling with a plastic bag: with murderous intentions. The two drifting men make a living by hauling rubbish – clothes, bidets, scrap metal – to the rubbish dump.

Jane Birkin finds the script 'Shakespearian: with the trio, the jealous man. Presumably I was completely amoral: I didn't think for a second that people would be that upset, because I understood the situation perfectly.' Gainsbourgian obsessions feature in the script: there is pissing, farting and fucking. The landfill is full of flies. Crows hit the windscreen, covering it in blood. Under the tank top of Jane/Johnny, we glimpse the outline of two nipples. She serves beers and hamburgers. And while she grabs the body and mouth of her future lover, at a Sunday dance that features a decadent strip-tease, Padovan gets beaten to pulp by some country boys – amongst them a pale-faced, long-haired Michel Blanc. In the early seventies, anti-gay segregation is still intense. And even if, in Frédéric Bonnaud's words, 'this very stylised film floats without being anchored, because we do not know where we are, or when' it does reflect its era.

Shot on a private airstrip near Uzès, the film centres on a prop: the bar, which is reminiscent of paintings by Edward Hopper or Andrew Wyeth. There is a string of cameos in the course of events: Nana, the touchingly ugly bullterrier bitch adored by Serge takes on the role of pillar of humanity in a world of misfits. And then Gérard Depardieu, brilliant, a pederast equipped with an outsized 'tool', sending his partners to hospital, which is why he has fallen in love with his horse. ('Alright, Pet!', he whispers, dishevelled, while licking the animal's ear – a classic scene). Krass quotes from Greek mythology, the Styx, the river of hell, 'that seeps along the filth to take it elsewhere'. And he buggers Johnny, Jane, a submissive boy. In February 2017, Jane Birkin was given a retrospective at the *Cinémathèque Française*; she didn't want to revisit *Je t'aime moi non plus*. She has reached the end of the road in her role as tireless advocate for Serge, all of Serge, including *Je t'aime moi non plus*. One can imagine why she didn't want to be in the audience at the *Cinémathèque*. She masturbates in the film. She offers herself, naked on an iron bed, to a guy who finds vaginas revolting. The worst thing about machos is that, even if that's what they are, they can't stand being called queer. But that's what she calls him and Krass/Dallesandro takes her violently from behind. She is hidden, crawling, curled up under the washbasin, repeating: 'I'm a boy, I'm a boy.' Gainsbourg films, he is in charge. Close-up, tracking shot, crotch, dust, groaning.

And each time they fuck – motels, tipper truck, landfill – she screams. So loudly that the motel owners call the police. He: 'Whores fuck in silence.' She: 'It's not my fault that it hurts.' ('That's how we lived, by the way,' Gainsbourg explains to Bayon on the subject of Jane.)

Jane harbours an intense loathing for the English journalist who wrote: 'Is Monsieur Gainsbourg not apprised of the use of butter?', in reference to Bertolucci's *Last Tango in Paris*. With hindsight, the actress Maria Schneider denounced the 'stick of butter' scene in which, as a nineteen year old, she is sodomised by a mature man, played by Marlon Brando. Even if there isn't any actual penetration, there is violence. The director, Bernardo Bertolucci, admitted in 2013 that he hadn't given Maria Schneider prior warning of the idea he'd had on the morning of the shoot – together with his fetish actor, who was then 48 – for a humiliating scene of sodomy with butter as lubricant.

On the occasion of a tribute to himself at the *Cinémathèque Française*, Bertolucci explained that he wanted to 'capture her reaction as a humiliated girl, for example when she screams "No, no." To make films, to obtain something, I think you have to be totally free sometimes. I didn't want Maria to act the humiliation, the rage; I wanted her to feel the humiliation and the rage. She has hated me all her life for this.' Maria Schneider took hard drugs and sank into chronic depression. The matter resurfaced in one of the newspapers in late 2016, after the suicide of the photographer David Hamilton; he was partial to blossoming young girls, whom he used as models and whom he dominated sexually. He liked the blond, Nordic type.

A culture of rape was hiding behind a culture of liberty at the time. *Don Juan 73* is a model of propriety in this respect. Bardot/Jeanne's mischief is anything but unbridled. At the height of the debauchery imagined by Vadim and Jean Cau, we are taken to Sweden, to the provincial university town of Lund, to which Jeanne drags her respectable lover, Pierre. Before the summer holidays, the students organise 'a kind of heathen carnival', the script explains: 'even though the standards of virtue are extremely loose, this isn't actually an orgy, but an explosion of life, which can manifest itself in many different ways.'

Serge Gainsbourg is a more radical filmmaker. What can we say about the on-set pictures taken by the set photographer Georges Pierre? Gainsbourg looking at Jane, naked, offered up on an iron bed; Gainsbourg showing his actors how to smother Jane by slipping a plastic bag over her head from behind. Gainsbourg, a cigarette hanging from his mouth, behind his cameraman and his soundman, together filming a sodomy scene with the absorption of an entomologist.

> I know that physical love is a dead end / I know it, but had I known it in time / I wouldn't have been, alas, the one you met,

Gainsbourg wrote for Jane, in the 1987 song 'Physique et sans issue' (Physical and Dead-end) ... Gainsbourg, with bulging eyes, is watching very closely as Joe Dallesandro kisses his wife – there are onset rumours that Jane is attracted to the handsome American, and vice versa, and that the Sorcerer's Apprentice is said to be jealous. '*No*,' – Jane takes exception to this.

'Serge was a tad in love with Joe. He was such a dream of a boy, and Hugues was perfect in his role of jealous lover. The nude scenes, which could have been a bit awkward, really weren't, because Joe was charming and not sleazy at all. It was a great team with Willy Kurant at the camera, Serge sublime, beautiful, the set photographer brilliant. The fuck scenes were very acrobatic, what with cables passing under our stomachs. As this was technically complicated, I just took care that nothing should be visible. I'd put adhesive tape here and there. And when it came to editing, I had total confidence in Serge.'

With a few exceptions, among them Henry Chapier, the film is not well received. The critic of the *Quotidien de Paris* writes: 'Thanks to its way of approaching the subject, without digression or coyness, *Je T'aime Moi Non Plus* is a film in the American idiom; it takes the risk of being at once misunderstood, unpopular, and in some ways iconoclastic. In Jane Birkin's tranquil career, this film is a gust of wind: the sharp, ravishing little English beauty knowingly squanders her capital of goodwill – which is based on the conventional image of the ingénue – in favour of a hellish role.'

The film is saved from an X rating – not to be shown to minors due to pornographic content – by the friendship of Michel Guy, then Secretary of State for Culture in the government of Valéry Giscard d'Estaing, who was elected, at 48, the 'youngest ever President of the Republic' in 1974. By the standards of the era – and let's not forget that Serge Gainsbourg always had his ear to the ground – *Je t'aime moi non plus* could have been indexed in the 'culture porn' category. Michel Guy and Valéry Giscard d'Estaing spent the first months after coming to power in giving France an image of modernity, of liberal mores. The porn movie is taking off and becomes a genre. Jean-François Davy directs *Exhibition* with Claudine Beccarie, the cult actress of the 'Golden Age of Porn'. The film is selected at Cannes. *Deep Throat* by Gerard Damiano, where the actress Linda Lovelace plays the role of a young woman whose clitoris is hidden in her throat, arrives from the United States.

But, at the end of 1975, as the filming of *Je t'aime moi non plus* is coming to an end, the government yields to pressure from family and Christian associations and introduces the 'X rating', crushing the porno under taxation to bring down independent production of these types of work. All this affects Serge Gainsbourg's first film.

Je t'aime moi non plus goes against the grain. Mores and public opinion are volatile. The film isn't widely distributed. Judy Campbell, Jane's mother, watches it in a cinema on the *Champs-Élysées*. 'She told me: "you are beautiful when you run with Nana," the dog. She was being stoic, because there were many sex scenes, too many in my humble opinion. The only fear I had was being suffocated by a plastic bag.' The critics are implacable. The self-righteous, and even some cinephiles, are irritated by the 'loud breathing' of the posterior coitus.

Delfeil de Ton, the leading light of the satirical magazine *Hara-Kiri* who has transitioned to *Libération*, considers the film boring. And 'sickening. Sickening, the exploitation of his wife Jane Birkin, who is reduced in the film, literally, to an arsehole who needs to be broken in. Sickening, the image of the other women in this film, meaning the scene with the strip-tease com-petition in the hangar. Women, Gainsbourg shows us, are just sad, flabby flesh that flaps and is limp.'

Madame Raymonde, Serge and Jane's 40-something help, washes the walls of the house at Rue de Verneuil every morn-ing: they are covered in graffiti that is obscene, menacing, or that question the director's virility. The director of photography, Willy Kurant, has to go back to the United States and shoot B-movies under the pseudonym Willy Kurtis. Gainsbourg finds solace in listening to François Truffaut predicting on the radio that *Je t'aime moi non plus* will end up in the film libraries.

Jane is under attack. In England, the film is shown in a single theatre, a gay cinema. Someone heckles her: "'And where did you put women's liberation?" Joe Dallesandro comes to my defence with his answer: "But she plays the role of a boy in the film!"' Laughter from the audience. Everything is heavy, everything is light.

'They said that Serge had turned me into trash. But no, the shoot was great, it was funny. Serge bent over backwards, he wanted everyone to be happy, he wanted parties. He had thought up the setting like an Edward Hopper painting. And we were happy to do whatever he asked of us. Every day, they braided my hair into very, very tight plaits, and then they put a short wig on me.' Jane, with hindsight, finds herself beautiful. 'It was one of the most beautiful pictures I ever had, because the tight wig pulled my eyes, because of the plaits.'

But Jane, who has conquered many hearts with her laugh, her charm, her romanticism, indeed takes a risk: that of no longer making people dream.

Jane – she's that little English girl, the companion of Alain Delon and Romy Schneider, the actress in Claude Zidi films like *I'm Losing My Temper* and *La Course à l'échalote* (Dirty Race), where she is partnered with Pierre Richard: 'She was as funny as she was beautiful' the latter writes in his autobiography. 'That's an understatement. She was open to anything, she put up with her hair being pulled, with being thrown in the mud, she was never afraid of ridicule … The more we tried to make her ugly, the more beautiful she became.' Jane and Serge, darlings of Saturday night, live in a storm of desire, a vortex of love and humiliation. Jane is an offering.

Hurt by the film's lack of success, Gainsbourg gets down to writing *L'Homme à tête de chou* (The Man with the Cabbage Head) after buying a work by the sculptress Claude Lalanne in a gallery near Rue de Verneuil. The metal statue shows a naked man with a huge cabbage instead of a head. Once again, Gainsbourg builds a scenario of his fantasies: a 40-year-old hack falls in love with a young shampoo girl, Marilou, who excites him as she dances to reggae. One night, coming home, he finds her between two

Macaques / Of the Woodstock-Festival type / She resembled a rock guitar / With two jacks: / One her mortar hole, the other her bullet hole.

He kills her with a fire extinguisher and ends up in a mental asylum.

Serge Gainsbourg has been odious at times, all the more so with Jane. She made a bargain. She was torn, which does not mean she could abide by it. 'She remained attached to a

Gainsbourgian sadomasochism,' Bayon explains. 'SM is always a contract, concluded by two individuals.' The one who breaks it forfeits the other. When Gainsbourg insults and hits her to make her reach emotional extremes in the recording studio – Tony Frank claims he witnessed scenes that ended in tears in the early seventies – Jane rises to the challenge. When, blind drunk, he wants to offer her up to the carnal desires of a provincial innkeeper, she detaches herself from the situation.

Gainsbourg heads, Gainsbourg tails. Jane white, Jane black. They are accomplices. He knows how to manipulate fantasies, which will place him at the apex of nonconformist, irreverent, subversive pop culture, with an allure that enrages some, while delighting others …

In 1971, Gainsbourg created 'La Décadanse': he whispers, the piano, harmonium-style, provides the slow dance tunes. The music video, directed by Jean-Christophe Averty, is steaming. Serge, Jane says, with a touch of innocence, feigned or otherwise, had invented a new dance: the man is behind the woman, so he 'can feel the woman's breasts with his hands in front of everyone on the dance floor; his idea was of an exquisite exhibitionism.' The backside rubbing against the prick of the man, 'that's wildly, wildly erotic, of all the songs we made together, this is one of my favourites, it stirs me much more than "Je t'aime … moi non plus". "*God for- / Give us our / Sins*", I found the words absolutely sublime, ecclesiastic, and, for us, not shocking.' 'It was revolutionary,' Jane explains. It was also a deplorable attempt at commercially recycling 'Je t'aime … moi non plus'.

In 1980, surrounded by the Jamaican musicians he has

recorded his reggae album with, Gainsbourg flips. He's a brute. The provocation that had helped him build his reputation becomes systematic. In 1979, he corrupts the 'Marseillaise'. A huge scandal ensues, a group of paras disrupt his concerts. Jane takes to the pen to insult Michel Droit, a member of the French Academy, who has written, in *Le Figaro Magazine*: that it's 'a profanation, pure and simple, of […] what is most sacred to us.' In passing, he has it in for Gainsbourg's 'incontinent eye' and 'drooling lip'.

The nature of the 'contract' between Jane and Serge changes when they split up. But it lasts. Birkin mentions this song from 1987, 'Une chose entre autres' (One Thing Among Others), 'the most truthful, a personal message, indeed, all the others as well, and everything he has written after our separation:

One thing among others / That you don't know /
You've had more than any other / The best of me.

Yes, this really seemed true to me, that I had the best of him. Until his death. He says: "Perfect journeys don't exist, don't worry, I've seen others, I'll get by with what I don't have." He moved on to other subjects. "You think I was going to retrace your steps, etc. But that's not going to happen; inside your head – who do you think you are?" It's a personal message, and at the same time a summary of our work since we no longer lived together. It's unbearable to have that many personal secrets revealed, interpreted, given away. And, at the same time, this was our life. At the same time this wasn't an oral pact, it wasn't spoken, it wasn't a promise, and all the same it's quite strange.'

Serge Gainsbourg in the registry office, marrying
Françoise (Béatrice) Pancrazzi on June 16, 1963 in Paris.

eighteen

Impedimenta and the outlines of the future

∙∙

*F*rom *Slogan*, where Jane is 'the little home wrecker', to *Don Juan*, where Brigitte Bardot is the sworn enemy of the couple in all its guises, marriage appears to be a hotbed of frustration, an obstacle to desire. Jane and Serge never got married. In 1971, Tony Frank photographs a mock wedding for *Mademoiselle Âge tendre*. They pose in Hyde Park, not far from Jane's London apartment in Chelsea. She: long white lace dress, with a wedding bouquet and a flower wreath in her hair. He: formal suit, frilly shirt cuffs and a large bow tie. 'They played the game. They were recording *Melody Nelson*,' Tony Frank relates. He was working at the studio with Jean-Claude Vannier. 'I went out to take pictures of Jane. It was a happy time.' These creative nuptials counted for more than the fantasy of everlasting marriage.

One thing is obvious: their union is a success. Two bodies unite and delight each other. Two families are joined together.

Lives are being built. But the exes still need dealing with, the inherited circumstances, so many *impedimenta*. A new love, or the radiant opportunity to shed one's burdens. Fear doesn't preclude danger, past experience doesn't preclude repetition, even if passion and grief have branded hearts and skins with a hot iron. Neither Jane, nor Serge are virginal creatures.

Jane has broken up with John Barry, her husband. Older than her, Gainsbourg knows more about grief and passion. In April 1989, Thierry Ardisson dedicates his programme *Lunettes noires pour nuits blanches* (Black Shades for White Nights) to Gainsbourg. A cult episode. This classic piece of television begins with an interview of Gainsbarre, in dark glasses: Gainsbarre by Gainsbourg, seen in a mirror. Gainsbarre's opening statement, wearing dark glasses: 'You look shit.' Then: 'Do you remember, in '47–48, the eight days you spent with Dali? With his salon covered with astrakhan?' Gainsbourg: 'Yes, I had the keys, he was in Cadaqués. I think that's why everything is black at my place, it was black at his. He had a mahogany shithouse, one might have imagined one was in the Raphael Rooms. I boned a girl on a square bed, three metres by three, I have the same at my place. On the floor, there were Mirós, Klees, Picassos, Dalís ... All of that left an impression on me for life, because there was a smell of sulphur, of excessive luxury.'

This version of events isn't quite correct. 'The girl' was his future wife. It was she to whom the Spanish painter had lent his apartment. A military conscript, Serge had come on leave and didn't dare to make love to her on the master's bed. Instead, they lived their passion on the furs covering the floor. Then,

Dali gave them a room that was covered with astrakhan. 'The girl', Élisabeth Levitzky, is a descendant of a particularly anti-Semitic aristocratic Russian family. Like Serge, she studies at the Beaux-Arts, and at the Montmartre academy of painting. Very pretty, she is a model and secretary to the poet, Georges Hugnet. She attends courses in Lucien Lelong suits. She leaves Gainsbourg speechless. She reads Simone de Beauvoir, belongs to the communist party and hangs out with artists.

When he takes her to the door of the boarding house she is staying in, he's dying to go further. But, at nineteen, he's still an adolescent – paralysed by shyness. So she kisses him. He sits down next to her, puts down his guitar, switches off the light and makes love to her seven times in a row. In November 1951, they get married. Lucien Ginsburg, the painter, writes his first song, 'Lili':

You're not pretty-pretty / And I risked my life for you,

but it's not clear who he's talking about – Lili is the diminutive of Élisabeth, but also that of Liliane, Serge's twin sister.

In October 2009, *Paris Match* publishes an amazing interview with Élisabeth Levitzky, who has just written an explosive book of memoirs, *Lise et Lulu, quarante ans d'amour* (Lise and Lulu, Forty Years of Love). Her words are like cutlasses. 'I am a Russian immigrant, like Serge. We are not even twenty. We fall madly in love. I'm against marriage, but, on 3 November 1951, I end up giving in. Wrongly. Luckily, we separate, on 9 October 1957. When we met, in 1947, we swore by nothing but free love and painting. But everything goes topsy-turvy at the end of Lulu's military service. He comes back a sniper and, most of all, hell-bent on marrying me. In 1951, I marry him, dressed in black; the only witnesses are the cook, and an instructor from Champsfleur – the school for Jewish orphans who have survived the concentration camps – where he teaches. Two days later, I walk in on Lulu with the school's laundry maid! Having forced marriage on me, he thus made me suffer his affairs, while preventing me from having my own. On paper, our marriage lasts six years. In reality, it is broken as soon as it is celebrated.'

Élisabeth Levitzky earns her own living. But, a married woman, she finds it intolerable to ask for her husband's permission to open a bank account. And yet that's what the law requires. It will only be in 1965 that the notion of 'head of the household' will be erased from the legal statutes, and the wife will be able to receive her dues without marital consent.

For Élisabeth and Serge, the marital cocktail is explosive. 'Nothing remains of the independent woman I was, of the free couple we were, even of our passion for painting,' Élisabeth adds. 'What's more, he makes me clear away my brushes. He hasn't touched his own in a long time. He goes out every night and sleeps ever more often at his mother's place. Eventually, we decide to separate.'

The portrait of Gainsbourg Élisabeth paints in her memoirs is cutting: 'He went to brothels, to see whores and to play the whore. The two women in his life are his mother and his daughter Charlotte. In the meantime, he had affairs.' Gainsbourg was, according to Élisabeth Levitzky, a man who needed a harem. He has often alluded to his quest for an 'overdose of fucking'.

What women fall for, she continues, is 'his painter's gaze', an expression of extreme alertness. As soon as he directed it at a woman, she let herself be seduced, she was in a trap, 'like a butterfly on a pin, and he paints her. He is very attentive. I have never known anyone as intent on giving pleasure, on having such an egalitarian relationship with a woman. No high-handed gesture, not one superfluous word, no coarseness.' She can tolerate his indiscretions, but not his renunciation of painting. She is convinced until the end that he could have been a great artist.

On the day of their divorce, Élisabeth confesses, they come to an agreement. Serge breaks an empty champagne bottle, they cut their wrists and mix their blood. At each break-up, the 'little Russian Jew' calls Élisabeth, the aristocrat. They swear that they will always be available for each other. Ten years after their separation, Élisabeth visits him at his studio at the *Cité Internationale des Arts* ('the CIA', as he put it), where there is a coming and going of his conquests. 'Our relationship is free, it is a relationship of pleasure. Each change of address is a pretext for an erotic inauguration. When he comes to my shop, at Rue des Canettes, I draw the curtains and we go down to the cellar, away from prying eyes. Over the years, my body has changed. I have grown fat, and thus taboo. We share a secret, and it's delightful.' When Jane Birkin leaves him, Élisabeth helps him to 'contain his rage and despair ... For almost 40 years, we have lived in "post-marital adultery", as he said.'

'Lili's' book is shunned by the keepers of the flame. Juliette Gréco, the artist keeping her own secrets, calls it 'an infamy'. The events Levitzky alludes to cannot be verified. What is not in doubt, however, is the disaster of Gainsbourg's second marriage, to Françoise Pancrazzi. She is the ex-wife of Georges Galitzine, scion of a famous Russian princely family. An industrialist's daughter, she had kept the title 'Princess Galitzine' thanks to her first husband. For Gainsbourg, she represents the kind of upper class that dazzles him; and that she has turned her back on. But Françoise hates her given name, calls herself Béatrice instead. She is also terribly jealous. The first scene, caused by a phone call, occurs on the day of the wedding, in 1964. 'She couldn't accept this profession, the many encounters it entailed [...] I understood immediately that this was going to turn into a nightmare. In any case, I'd been right to organise the wedding dinner at a Russian restaurant: the atmosphere it took place in was absolutely Siberian.'

Régine turns up in curlers and, with a certain amount of humour, reassures her friend Serge's wife. With Juliette Gréco, it's a different story. Imperious, the singer sees Béatrice arrive one day, when Gainsbourg is working at her place. 'She was magnificent, but her eyes were like embers. Gainsbourg pursued by this murderous panther was a sight to behold. She was ready to gun everyone down. How dramatic! Mind you, I can understand that one might get jealous over such a man ...' For work sessions with a partner, he arranges to meet at his father's, not at Rue Tronchet, where the couple inhabit an opulent apartment. 'My wife can't bear it when another woman comes to see me at home. It generally goes badly and ends in drama.'

And yet, seven months after Serge and Béatrice's wedding, their daughter, Natacha Pancrazzi-Ginsburg, is born at the height of the *yé-yé* craze. Gainsbourg faces paternity and success. Groupies sleep on his doorstep. The stars are free and unattached. In *Gainsbourg confidentiel* (Gainsbourg Confidential), Pierre Mikaïloff relates that in 1963, Serge Gainsbourg acts opposite Dalida on the set of *The Stranger of Hong Kong*, by Jacques Poitreneaud. Convinced that he is cheating on her with Dalida, Béatrice jumps on a plane to Hong Kong, knocks on the singer's door and slaps her, before going back to Paris. Serge Gainsbourg leaves Béatrice in 1966. They divorce. He briefly returns to their marital home, the time it takes to conceive a son and to escape into the arms of Brigitte Bardot. Paul is born in the spring of 1968, when Serge has just met Jane.

When Jane leaves him, twelve years later, he will suffer and be reborn. His worsening health and bloated face do not prevent him from seducing Bambou, a magnificent Eurasian lioness, an archetypal oriental fantasy. He drinks, she shoots smack, and he prevents her from committing suicide. They even have a child: Lucien is born in 1986. The Princess Galitzine seizes Natacha and Paul. Jane, on the contrary, will let Serge take Charlotte into the limelight. In 1984, Gainsbourg shocks his public by recording 'Lemon Incest', a pun on the words 'zest' and 'incest'; which he sings as a duet with Charlotte, who is then twelve years old. In the video, the girl wears a skimpy nightie, in bed with her topless father, who evokes 'the love we will never make to each other', describing it as 'the most unique, the most intoxicating'. The music is inspired by Frédéric Chopin's 'Étude n° 3, Opus 10'. Gainsbourg's word on the subject was: 'I have skimmed the surface of incest. Full stop. Not deflowered it.'

Serge during the filming of the television show 'Neither fig nor grape'.

nineteen

Éros, Thanatos, women's bodies and voices: supreme object of desire

. . . .

'*I* drown before my mirror, because I can't swim. These are troubled waters, dangerous marshlands. Some see a heavenly reflection; for me, it's a miasma,' Gainsbourg confessed to Yves Salgues. He added, in a bruised, cocky manner that, had he been better-looking, he would have died of exhaustion. For him, women are something unfathomable that he seeks to capture. A painter before he was a singer, he develops an art of seduction that took him into the arms of some very pretty girls. 'I've had some real stunners; I took them, and they took off,' sighed Gainsbarre: a fantasised version of Lucien Ginsburg: the scumbag edition.

Gainsbourg is physically unattractive. At first glance, Jane Birkin had found him sinister, even sadistic. But some gorgeous women, including Brigitte Bardot and Juliette Gréco, saw his beauty. In the early sixties, Gainsbourg is all choreography: hands flying, eyes turning, elbows pointed, legs thrust out. He wears a tie and a white shirt to compensate for 'the shiver of rejection' that was often palpable among the audiences of the cabarets where he appeared – an oddball with large ears, withdrawn into a studied arrogance. 'I move in alcoves of snobbery. I don't write "the song that tears down walls on sweating pavements",'* explains Gainsbourg in reference to his art.

'The reception he was given – I'd seen the same thing happen to Boris Vian: it's a mixture of hatred and fascination,' relates Alain Goraguer, Gainsbourg's arranger from 1958 to 1963; they knew each other from the club *Milord l'Arsouille*. 'One could almost read the audience's thoughts, even when rude comments like: "You look shit and your singing is lousy" weren't bursting forth directly from the crowd. Neither Vian nor Gainsbourg exuded any charm.'** Jane Birkin extricates Gainsbourg from his glacial period.

Gainsbourg lived at 5, Rue de Verneuil in Paris, exactly opposite the practice of the psychoanalyst Jacques Lacan. Having learned the art of dodging, he was never psychoanalysed: according to Lacan, author of *Écrits* (Writings): 'where there is talking, there is pain.' The psychoanalyst Michel David, author of *Serge Gainsbourg, la scène du fantasme*, relates that what interests Gainsbourg is the experience of pleasure – at a

----

* The quote is a skewed allusion to *Le Bruit des Cabarets, le Fange des Trottoirs* (The Noise of the Cabarets, the Mire of the Streets) by Paul Verlaine.

** Catherine Schwaab, 'Gainsbourg, *serial lover*', *Paris Match*, March 2016.

time when pleasure, for a woman, is still considered sinful. This is not simple; in fact, it could even be considered as a twisted path. 'Woman does not exist' Jacques Lacan had proclaimed at a famous seminar in 1970–71, on the subject of the 'Semblant'.*
All women who are anatomically women don't combine into one woman, Lacan pointed out, ahead of later gender theories. Gainsbourg is certainly misogynous. Like his neighbour in Saint-Germain-des-Prés, he knows that seduction is all about appearances: 'feminine masquerade, masculine swagger.' He thinks that equality goes no further than the foot of the bed. Not for the reasons one might assume, because – like Lacan – he has identified the impalpable: there isn't just one sexual pleasure, there are two: the one, phallic, shared pleasure and the other, unfathomable, elusive, which can't be put into words.

Serge Gainsbourg's sexual life begins with the services of prostitutes in Barbès, and his amorous life with a fantasy expressed in waves, unfurled on the beach at Trouville, during the summer of 1938. Loudspeakers emit the music of Charles Trenet: *I have your hand in my hand / I play with your fingers*, while an eight-year-old blonde called Béatrice with braided hair and freckles on her shoulder, who is staying nearby with her family, passes by his side. The die is cast. It is the voice that is the most beautiful sexual organ. Jean-Luc Godard shares this interest in it: he got his wife Anna Karina to sing, and later the

---

* A Lacanian concept. Put simply, a Semblant resembles an object/person/ behaviour in which a subject takes pleasure, partly because it is only a resemblance.

young *yé-yé* Chantal Goya, heroine of his 1966 film *Masculin féminin* (Masculine Feminine: Fifteen Specific Events), which is 'obviously banned for minors, since it deals with their experiences' as the master of the French New Wave proclaims in the trailer. He also (while Gainsbourg is emancipating himself from French *chanson* by writing 'Qui est in, qui est out') unequivocally writes 'MAS – CUL – IN Féminin' across the screen. The woman is whole, the man in pieces.

'The genius of Gainsbourg lies in the creation of this superior entity: a woman's vocal destiny,' writes Yves Salgues. Serge Gainsbourg's erotic life cuts across his art. He makes songs in which innocence is tainted by perversion. To have them performed, he seeks sensuality in the voice. As Mireille Darc (who also sings for him) sums up: 'He wagered everything on breath,' on distress, on unspoken attraction. Jean-Claude Brialy acted and sang in Gainsbourg's musical *Anna*: 'When he writes for someone, he needs to be a little bit in love with that person. He even told me he was in love with me!' Mischievous, this Brialy, but not very talented: he needed Serge's voice as support for his own, in order not to go off the tracks.

Gainsbourg didn't take much interest in *bourgeois* women, with the possible exception of Michèle Arnaud, a snobbish, distinguished singer, the wife of Francis Claude, owner of the *Milord l'Arsouille*. It is she who discovers that Ginsburg the painter and pianist is also a writer of songs. And when she sings

'La femme des uns sous le corps des autres' (The Wife of Some Under the Body of Others), she arouses Lucien's desires. He likes chic eccentrics. He is a misogynist, or claims to be, and is at the mercy of beautiful women. Juliette Gréco, for example. Faced with her, he goes to pieces, knocks his coffee cup over, is speechless. He writes 'Il était une oie' (Once There Was a Goose), an ambiguous, derisive and feminist song for her. In the contradictory reactions of attraction and rejection that women inspire in him, Gréco perceives lucidity: 'He's just telling the truth, he doesn't have the least meanness within him.' Before adding, acidly: 'He had every talent, except maybe one for happiness.' Juliette Gréco continues: 'I have been terrified by his shyness. It was terrible to see a man in such a state of fragility, of embarrassment and anxiety. He then wrote some very beautiful songs for me, among them "La Javanaise", which, by the way, took some time to find its audience. I insisted, until it became, in a way, Gainsbourg's *Marseillaise* – famous all over the world.'

Gainsbourg's songs were mostly sung by women. The performers: Juliette Gréco, Catherine Sauvage, Françoise Hardy, France Gall, Petula Clark, Zizi Jeanmaire, Régine, Vanessa Paradis … He is fixated on actresses: Anna Karina, fabulous in the televised version of *Anna* (1967), Bardot, Deneuve, Adjani. 'He makes them sing very close to the microphone, one can almost hear them breathe. Listen to Catherine Deneuve in 'Dieu est un fumeur de havane' (God is a Smoker of Havanas),' Jane Birkin says, perceptively.

Gainsbourg loved Billie Holiday for her flaws and couldn't stand singers with powerful voices, preferring Judy Garland to her daughter Liza Minnelli. He has never written a song for Édith Piaf. 'You need throaty songs, songs that come from the gut; I just play with words,' he'd explained to the indomitable giant of the *chanson*. He loved actresses for their frailty, their lack of self-confidence. From Michèle Mercier to Mireille Darc, he wanted them all. He was seeking their emotionality. 'When something broke, when emotions boiled over, he didn't care about the words,' Birkin says. The *chanson* may be a minor art, but it is an amorous one, with a zest of perversion to boot.

Gainsbourg knows this – he who has written 'Les Sucettes' (Lollipops) for France Gall, after 'Poupée de cire, poupée de son', which won the 1965 Eurovision Song Contest, and the very *yé-yé* song 'Laisse tomber les filles' (Let Go of the Girls). The lollipops are clearly a metaphor for fellatio, but young France, eighteen at the time, doesn't get it. Gainsbourg is delighted and gains a new reputation: as that of a Manichaean provocateur. France Gall remains in her blonde innocence and thinks of the barley sugar that takes her to paradise 'when nothing but the little stick remains on her tongue.' As an adult, eventually married to Michel Berger, wrapped up as part of a happy couple that sells records like hotcakes, she refused to even speak to Gainsbourg. Some time later, on television, he softens a bit vis-à-vis Michel Berger and tells him that 'France Gall has saved my life' by introducing him to a circle of celebrity that had hitherto been closed to him. With the *yé-yé* craze, a mass phenomenon develops: groupies force their way backstage, sleep on the singer's doorstep, wait for him to return from his nocturnal adventures at dawn. All this can go to one's head.

Of course, there had been BB. But Bardot the singer had been around before Gainsbourg. Since he couldn't mould her, he dressed her. From the beginning, BB the dancer loves to sing – in 1956, in Vadim's ... *And God Created Woman*, she can be heard humming 'Je suis une croqueuse de diamants' (I Am a Diamond-eater) by Zizi Jeanmaire, or 'Moi j'm'en fous, j'm'en contrefous' (I Don't Care, I Really Don't Give a Damn) by Yves Montand. In 1962, she signs her debut single, which includes 'Sidonie', a poem by Charles Cros, put to music by Jean-Max Rivière and Yannis Spanos; she sings it while accompanying herself on the guitar, in the film *A Very Private Affair* by Louis Malle:

Because for her, being naked / Is her prettiest dress / Everyone knows / That Sidonie has more than one lover.

In 1963 Philips releases the album *Brigitte Bardot Sings*, featuring 'La Madrague' by Jean-Max Rivière and Gérard Bourgeois, and 'L'Appareil à sous', which Gainsbourg, still unscarred by love, has written for her. In 1965, he gives her 'Bubble Gum'.

The year 1967 spawns many love affairs. Jane hasn't yet joined the party. A few months before the passionate affair with Bardot, there was this fragile but never-breaking beauty, this face of haunted innocence, this black voice with a Nordic accent: Anna Karina. Gainsbourg wanted to write a musical, and chose the Dane after hearing her sing in Jean-Luc Godard's film *Pierrot le Fou*. Charm works its magic, one feels it through-out *Anna*, which is filmed for television by the director Pierre Koralnik, and particularly in a memorable slow-dance: 'Ne dis rien' (Say Nothing), a duet she and Gainsbourg sing as they hold each other's gaze:

> Follow me to the end of the night, to the end of my folly.

'At the time, Serge Gainsbourg was very restrained, very well dressed, all that …' Anna Karina explained in 2013, during the theatrical revival of *Anna*, with Cécile de France in the lead role. '"Sous le soleil exactement" [Precisely Under the Sun], that was so revolutionary! We worked at his place. He lived at a studio, somewhere on the Right Bank, with nothing but a grand piano in it. He was terribly shy, playful, very elegant, and already cyni-cal. The atmosphere was fantastic. It was a godsend: I'd always wanted to be in a musical. Gainsbourg was a perfectionist. We spoke in pig Latin, talked rubbish. We ate cheese and drank red wine. I've hardly ever had as much fun with a man as I did with Serge. I lost him, because he met BB, then Birkin.' With Brialy, they film on the huge beach at Deauville. 'I lost him …' Anna Karina confides, because there was a snag: Godard – whom she had married in 1961 when she was twenty and he ten years older. 'I was getting over a marriage with one legend and I couldn't love another.'

Godard had discovered Anna Karina in an ad for 'Monsavon', pretending to be naked in a bathtub, covered in soap bubbles. She refuses to appear 'in the buff' in his film *À bout de souffle*. She falls in love with him, becomes his fetish actress, appears in seven of his films, from *The Little Soldier* to *Made in USA*. And it's hell! The actress has attempted suicide four times and spent time in a psychiatric hospital. She is exhausted. In Jean-Claude Brialy's words: 'They tore each other to pieces, fought, screamed at each other … Then the storm was over and we continued to have fun.' Godard is in search of *the* great love, in the style of Orson Wells and Rita Hayworth, thinks he is entitled to it. His friend, the actor Antoine Bourseiller, sees in him a man who is 'painfully imprisoned in his romanticism, which he dissimulates with rage, as if it were a cancer.' Anna Karina and Jean-Luc Godard break up. In July 1967, the master of the New Wave marries Anne Wiazemsky, granddaughter of the novelist François Mauriac. Anna Karina, for her part, takes flight.

Is Gainsbourg depraved? He's certainly a player. His toy in 1969, this year of erotic vintage, is Jane Birkin's voice, which flows in a trickle, fragile and trembling. 'The marvel with Jane,' he explained to Yves Salgues, 'consisted in her weakness: her voice couldn't be controlled. She couldn't even pretend to control it. What she could do was to work without trying to force things against her nature. The one thing she has always been good at is expressing herself through her voice. That's why she gives the high-school kids goosebumps. Each time she opens her mouth, we feel that she is defending herself against a maniac, or a criminal.' Jane, he continues, 'is the tragic actress of a choice repertoire' – chosen by him: who has 'dressed her voice to measure'.

But isn't it the other way round? The macho society of the post-war years attributes genius to the man, and to the woman: the work of a seamstress. Serge was everything to Jane. Or almost everything. But what did she give him? What did she offer him, her masculine-feminine alter ego? What, in turn, did this tormented and funny man, with whom she has shared 'the twelve most beautiful years' of his life, offer her? After his encounter with Jane Birkin, Serge Gainsbourg, already the author of some classics of French *chanson* – 'Le Poinçonneur des Lilas', 'La Javanaise', 'Les Sucettes', 'Les P'tits Papiers' – has written his most accomplished albums: *Histoire de Melody Nelson*, *L'Homme à tête de chou*, *Rock Around the Bunker*. She sang them with talent, dressing and undressing Serge's oeuvre, interpreter of the works of a 'major poet' from the moment when, in 1969, he first dedicates an album to her: *Serge Gainsbourg / Jane Birkin*.

He writes marvels for her, from 'Jane B.' to 'Amours des feintes', which was released nine years after their separation.

Separation and death notwithstanding: Jane carries the songs of her companion in life and in art, written while they were still together, or beyond their conflicts, thanks to the unfailing strength of their bond. 'It is a privilege that one of the greatest French songwriters has written for me, from when I was twenty to when I was 45. You see, it never stopped. It's a strange situation. What can I do for him now, when it's too late? At least I can carry him, take him with me. Say his words!'

Jane Birkin and Serge Gainsbourg photographed in 1979, shortly before their relationship came to an end.

twenty

The night belongs to us

•••

*O*n this evening in June, there's a concert at the *Salo Club*. A stone's throw from the Stock Exchange, this Parisian club has recently changed its name: it used to be called *Social Club*, but swapped its electro merrymaking for a more esoteric format and a bit of underground. *Salò, or the 120 Days of Sodom* comes to mind – Pier Paolo Pasolini's ultra-trashy film where denunciation of Mussolini's fascism meets the orgies of the Marquis de Sade. At the foot of the stairs is a succession of small vaults, leading to a narrow stage covered with graffiti, low ceilings and lights that wouldn't look out of place in a squat from the alternative-rock era. Paint is peeling off the concrete: a reclaimed aesthetic.

It is hot; vodka is served on ice, in plastic cups. There is no VIP area here. One mixes. You're not even obliged to listen to the musicians who are playing. You could also retreat to a lounge bathed in purple light, where Marlene Dietrich appears on a plasma screen. The boys chat up girls who drink beers straight from the bottle. Together they chase rainbows to planet party. But tonight, it is Dani who is majestic.

She's decked out in leather: boots with high heels and bling, a pendant with spread eagle wings. A contortionist has taken up residence at the bar in the rear, working towards the deconstruction of the body; her gaze is empty and distant. She toils away. At the same time, at the foot of the stage, there are catcalls: 'Hey! What's wrong with you; what do you want; you always have that look … if your life's out of order, fix it.'

Dani has started a band consisting of girls only. Katel is at the bass, Marie Lalonde, daughter of the former Green Party leader and presidential candidate Brice, plays the second guitar, there's a drummer in bermudas, boy-scout socks, a crew cut and piercings. Groovy. She met the girls in connection with a tribute album for the singer Barbara, where she covered her 'Si la photo est bonne' (If the Photo is Good) in a hazy rock style.

Born in 1944, Dani has written a brilliant book, *La nuit ne dure pas* (The Night Won't Last) – with the same title as the album that rekindled her career. Muse of Parisian nights after working with Vadim (*Circle of Love* in 1964), filming with Truffaut (*Day for Night*) and appearing in one of the New-Wave-era magazines, she ran the hugely fashionable nightclub *L'Aventure* on Avenue Victor Hugo. Then she took to drugs in a big way. Resurfacing from heroin use, she opened a shop selling roses, *Au nom de la rose*; the brand was exploited to her detriment by her business partners.

Serge Gainsbourg has written a wonderful song for her: 'Comme un boomerang' (Like a Boomerang).

I feel a boom and a bang / Stirring in my injured heart / Love, just like a boomerang / Returning from days gone past / All to cry the crazy tears / Of the body I'd given to you.

In 1974, Dani and Gainsbourg conceived, rehearsed and designed the song at Rue de Verneuil, surrounded by Kate and Jane, who was holding Charlotte in her arms. They wanted to present it at Eurovision, ten years after 'Poupée de cire, poupée de son'. Hardly in line with the standards of the contest, 'Comme un boomerang' was refused.

In 2001, Étienne Daho covers the song in a duet with Dani and it's a massive success. Daho, the godfather of French pop, in love with London, is a stalwart friend: he works with those he loves – Françoise Hardy, and Jeanne Moreau on the musical adaptation of 'Le Condamné à mort' (The Man Condemned to Death) by Jean Genet. Daho loves duets with women. In 2003, the dandy from Rennes hires Charlotte Gainsbourg to sing one of his compositions, 'If', with him. Another big hit! He also writes for Jane and produces an album for Lou Doillon. Daho is a family friend. He has accompanied Serge and Jane on their Bohemian escapades.

This evening in June 2017, while Dani signs her book at the entrance, Étienne Daho is there, jeans and a T-shirt, a drink in his hand; he looks tired but happy, because he has just finished his new album. Next to him, Lou Doillon, vodka on ice. Lou Doillon is absolutely her own person. A staunch feminist, she reels off in detail the macho fixations of rock bands and the outrage they provoke in her. Together we decipher the graffiti on the backstage walls. Where are the women? The misogynist covers his face, says that he loves women, just as the racist keeps saying that he has a black friend. They, the women, are music's negroes. Some have revolted, of course: edgy Marianne Faithfulls, raving Asia Argentos, intractable Brigitte Fontaines.

Lou Doillon is as straight as the letter I, has cascading hair and she knows what's what. 'It's time to turn the tide,' she says. As a matter of fact, it is right to ask what Jane gave to Serge, and not vice versa. On this subject, she agrees entirely with Jane: 'What my mother gave Serge is femininity: the little beard, the moccasins and jewellery.' Which is essential. Yes, says Étienne Daho, that's correct. He knows what he is taking about. More than that, since he has 'really lived with them for five years, days, nights, everything.' But the reserved and bright young man had his own theory on celebrity.

Even if celebrity entails a permanent *mise-en-scène*, even if dominating the newspapers, television screens and social media is mandatory, even if fame requires the continuous reinvention of one's persona, it cannot exist without desire. In order to keep this desire alive, there needs to be 'mystery', Étienne keeps telling me. 'One should never express everything.' Never reveal what could break the spell of the fans' fantasy. That's an iron law in this business.

Moreover, revelation is a 'machine that produces banality'. It destroys. Because it might expose lives that are, after all, normal: going to bed early, instant coffee-substitute in the morning, gym in the afternoon, walks with the dog. Or, conversely, trashy scenes, with serious flaws and depravity. Revelation enfeebles, it should be banished. The crowd is dreaming. It doesn't want to know about the limitations of Johnny Hallyday. Nor about the drug addiction of the beloved comedian Coluche. Nor the venality of Jean-Jacques Goldman.* The public is always right. It is entitled to cheer Renaud** when he is incapacitated and to ensure his success when he can no longer carry a tune. It has every right to think it's great when the rapper Chris Brown gets a tattoo of his girlfriend Rihanna's disfigured face after beating her black and blue.

The acknowledgement of homosexuality, for example, is only possible posthumously, because the girls dream of Prince Charming and the boys fantasize about the sexy attitudes of the starlets. From Freddy Mercury to Françoise Sagan, everything was kept quiet until the funeral.

Who can take the measure of the crazy power that celebrity, wealth or influence can bestow?

The sexual escapades engaged in with sex objects, silly, inebriated groupies gathered backstage, or in stars' houses, are commonplace. They come to light via a court case, the kind epitomised by that of Polanski, who was accused of drugging a thirteen-year-old girl in order to fuck her. Those who really want to can discover the world of showbiz via the memoirs authored by giants of the business who no longer have anything

---

* France's highest-earning singer-songwriter after Johnny Hallyday, formerly with the trio Fredericks Goldman Jones.

** Gravelly-voiced French balladeer, singer of many modern classics, most famous outside of France for 'Miss Maggie'.

to fear, such as Keith Richards. But how can we reveal the full story without being authorised to do so?

Dani told us that a respected newspaper wrote one day that she was shooting smack. Her children read the article: it was terrible, because it wasn't true. She got high by snorting excessive amounts of heroin. But she never injected herself. This makes all the difference but who, outside the inner circle, appreciates the value of such details? And how to demand an accurate reading for those who are skinned alive?

In 2003, for *Cahiers du cinéma*, France Gall rejoined Jean-Luc Godard, whom she had asked to direct the video clip for 'Plus haut' (Higher), a song that was written by her husband, Michel Berger, who was a regular at Eddie Barclay's white parties. He died at Barclay's house, Domaine de la Capilla, in Ramatuelle, in 1992. Gall, the star of francophone entertainment and former muse of Serge Gainsbourg during his malicious period, explains to the master of the New Wave: 'People want to know you, to unravel the mystery, try to pinpoint your personality, while everything in this business is geared towards alienating you, putting you on a pedestal. The stage that's well above their heads, the lighting ... Everything is designed to keep you apart. That's why they love it when one talks about oneself through a song.'

In 1965, Gainsbourg wrote 'Poupée de cire, poupée de son' for the young Gall:

> My records are mirrors / In which everyone can see me / I am everywhere at once / Broken into a thousand shards of my voice.

Protected by Jane, Serge is now beyond reach. Here and there, one digs up plausible explanations of events. Drunk, Gainsbourg gets heavy, he wants to pick up a young woman. Her boyfriend has different ideas, so the singer gets a punch in the face. The black eye is a badge of honour. There is something obsessive in the disgraceful way Gainsbarre treats the drugged-out Bambou when he meets her. Who else but Charlotte Gainsbourg could have described her father's dead body, a leg sticking out beneath the blanket? Would the question even be admissible if she hadn't written a song about it, 'Lying With You', the ultimate attempt to reappropriate the grief the crowd had taken from her?

Jane and Serge have lived when neither the music or cinema industry had yet spawned the cold monsters who write a song with a team of a hundred contributors. They were at liberty to disclose the truth of their love, in a nakedness that was touching, while spreading it all over the magazines, the television, the radio, the cinema – everywhere.

At the *Salo Club*, the vodka bottles in the private booths have been emptied. Not by us. Dani is being sensible, and Lou, a mother and housewife, has to get up early the next day. We have one for the road and it's a sweet moment. The girls in our group smoke outside. It's one in the morning. For them, the night is young. Paris is a spectacle of Ubers with tinted windows. Fast cars have definitely disappeared from the Parisian night. *Spitfire go home*.

Bibliography

The quotations contained in this book are based on interviews given to the author, on publications quoted in the text, as well as the following publications:

Serge Gainsbourg

Dernières Nouvelles des étoiles: paroles des chansons (song lyrics), Paris, Plon/Pocket, 1999.

Pensées, provocs et autres volutes: extraits d'interviews et paroles des chansons (interview extracts and song lyrics), Paris, Le Livre de Poche, 2007.

L'Intégrale et cætera (complete lyrics), Yves-Ferdinand Bouvier and Serge Vincendet, Paris, Bartillat, 2009.

Les Manuscrits de Serge Gainsbourg: chansons, brouillons et inédits (songs, drafts and unpublished work), Laurent Balandras, Paris, Textuel, 2011.

Other publications.

Gainsbourg: The Biography, Gilles Verlant, TamTam Books, 2012.

Gainsbourg et cætera, Gilles Verlant and Isabelle Salmon, Vade Retro, 1994.

Gainsbourg, Gilles Verlant and Jean-Dominique Brierre, Paris, Albin Michel, 2000.

Serge Gainsbourg, la scène du fantasme, Michel David, Arles, Actes Sud, 1999.

Gainsbourg sans filtre, Marie-Dominique Lelièvre, Paris, Flammarion, 2008.

Gainsbourg ou la Provocation Permanente, Yves Salgues, Paris, Le Livre de Poche, 1998.

Serge Gainsbourg, mort ou vices, interviews with Bayon, Paris, Grasset, 1992.

Lise et Lulu, Lise Levitzky and Bertrand Dicale, First, 2010.

Recherche jeune homme aimant le cinéma: souvenirs, Pierre Grimblat, Paris, Grasset, 2008.

Moi, mes histoires, Régine, Monaco, Éditions du Rocher, 2006.

Brigitte Bardot. La femme la plus belle et la plus scandaleuse au monde, Yves Bigot, Paris, Don Quichotte, 2014.

Initiales B.B., Brigitte Bardot, Paris, Grasset, 1996.

D'une étoile l'autre, by Roger Vadim, Edition No. 1, 1990.

J'inventais ma vie, vol. I: Madame Arthur, Marie-Pierre Pruvot (Bambi), Plombières-les-Bains, Ex Aequo, 2012.

Tout Gainsbourg, Bertrand Dicale, Paris, Jungle, 2016.

Jane Birkin, Frédéric Quinonero, Paris, L'Archipel, 2016.

DVD

Slogan by Pierre Grimblat, with bonus tracks, interviews with Pierre Lescure, Frédéric Beigbeder, Pierre Grimblat.

Jane Birkin/Serge Gainsbourg: Discography

Fontana:

1969: *Jane Birkin – Serge Gainsbourg*

1971: *Histoire de Melody Nelson*

1973: *Di Doo Dah*

1975: *Lolita Go Home*

1978: *Ex-Fan des Sixties*

Philips:

1983: *Baby Alone in Babylone*

1987: *Lost Song*

1990: *Amours des feintes*

1996: *Versions Jane*

Parlophone:

2017: *Birkin Gainsbourg: le symphonique.*

Live albums:

1987: *Jane Birkin at the Bataclan*

1992: *Je suis venue te dire que je m'en vais …* (concert at Casino de Paris)

2002: *Arabesque*

2009: *Au Palace*

2012: *Jane Birkin sings Serge Gainsbourg via Japan*

Filmographie Birkin / Gainsbourg

1969: *Slogan*, by Pierre Grimblat

1969: *The Pleasure Pit*, by André Cayatte

1970: *French Intrigue*, by Pierre Koralnik

1976: *Je t'aime moi non plus*, by Serge Gainsbourg

1988: *Jane B. par Agnès V.*, by Agnès Varda

2007: *Boxes*, by Jane Birkin

Acknowledgements

Jane Birkin, Régine, Étienne Daho, Brigitte Bardot, Olivier Gluzman, Bruno Bayon, Yves Bigot, Tony Frank, Philippe Lerichomme, Gilles Verlant (1957–2013), Capitol Music, Universal Music.

About the author

Véronique Mortaigne is a journalist – the author of several books on, among others, Cesaria Evora, Johnny Hallyday, and Manu Chao.